Modern life places a special emphasis on private affairs. Social institutions, and especially our economies, have been organized to facilitate the pursuit of private interests. At the center of this private world is a system of private property which, more than anything, satisfies our wants. Political economy studies the properties of this private world: How does it work, and how well does it satisfy our wants? What are the limits of the world of private affairs?

Wealth and Freedom provides an introduction to political economy for the student or other interested nonspecialist. The book explores such key issues as the place of our economy in the larger social system, the importance of market institutions for individual autonomy, private enterprise as a system of economic development, poverty and inequality in market economies, global inequality, and the limits of the market and the role of government. *Wealth and Freedom* is distinctive in employing a rights-based approach to understanding and evaluating economic institutions. The author emphasizes the distinction between needs and wants as the basis for establishing the limits of the market, and concludes the book with a discussion of the relation between private wants and public ends.

About the Author

MARILYN DANIELS is Associate Professor of Speech Communication at The Pennsylvania State University. She is the author of *Benedictine Roots in the Development of Deaf Education: Listening with the Heart* (Bergin & Garvey, 1997) and numerous articles in communication education journals.

Wealth and freedom

Wealth and freedom

An introduction to political economy

DAVID P. LEVINE
University of Denver

PUBLISHED BY THE PRESS SYNDICATE OF THE UNIVERSITY OF CAMBRIDGE
The Pitt Building, Trumpington Street, Cambridge CB2 1RP, United Kingdom

CAMBRIDGE UNIVERSITY PRESS
The Edinburgh Building, Cambridge CB2 2RU, United Kingdom
40 West 20th Street, New York, NY 10011-4211, USA
10 Stamford Road, Oakleigh, Melbourne 3166, Australia

First published 1995
Reprinted 1997

Printed in the United States of America

Typeset in Plantin

A catalogue record for this book is available from the British Library

Library of Congress Cataloguing-in-Publication Data is available

ISBN 0-521-44791-7 paperback

Contents

Figures and tables

Preface

This volume developed out of lectures I gave in an undergraduate core course taught over a number of years at the University of Denver. My experience with that course taught me something about the difficulties of teaching and learning and about the pitfalls of writing for the purpose of the general education of students.

In my core course I introduce students without background in economics to long-standing themes and ideas of political economy. Today, interest in issues of political economy runs high. The challenge in teaching is to translate an interest in issues into an interest in understanding the larger framework of economic life that spawns those issues.

As it turned out, the book is well suited for only a part of its original audience. Students, and readers more generally, vary in their interest in and patience with the broader concerns emphasized here. Those with an interest in the framework of our thinking about the economy, especially its place in the larger fabric of our social lives, should find this book of value.

In recent years the term political economy has taken on breadth and diversity as interest in the subject has grown substantially. This book does not attempt to mirror either the breadth or diversity of contemporary work in political economy. It speaks from only one of its corners – originally Adam Smith's, although in his day it was a larger part of the whole than it is today. The approach adopted here bears the influence of many economists who were inspired in different ways by the ideas of Smith and his great followers, especially Karl Marx and John Maynard Keynes.

In the following pages I introduce a way of thinking about the workings of a capitalist or private enterprise economy. I do not attempt to compare approaches or present doctrines. I am not of the belief that clear thinking develops well in a cacophony of point counterpoint. The main value this book has is for those interested in a connected narrative written within one (synthetic) framework. My hope is that, though it draws on different sources, it has the virtue of an integrated whole that might provide the reader with help in making sense of important issues.

Acknowledgments

I would like to thank a number of colleagues for their comments and suggestions on earlier drafts of this book: Robert Blecker, Harry Bloch, Jack Donnelly, Naeem Inayatullah, Tracy Mott, Jane Knodell, Carol Heim, Nina Shapiro, Nawfal Umari, and Pam Wolfe. Lee Repasch and Tom Scott provided valuable research assistance. Several anonymous readers provided helpful suggestions. I am also grateful to Emily Loose and Alex Holzman for their work on this project.

Introduction

The world we live in places special emphasis on private affairs. We have organized our social institutions, especially our economies, to facilitate the pursuit of private interests. In this world we think of the things we accomplish in our lives in a special way: They are primarily our own accomplishments, and they are meant to serve our private ends.

At the center of this private world is a system of private property. More than anything else, we need private property to satisfy our wants. The property system is one of producing, consuming, buying, and selling. This is the system we have come to refer to as our economy. It is a private property, private enterprise, market-centered economy.

Political economy studies the properties of this private world: How does it work, and how well does it satisfy our wants? What does it mean to us, and how does it form our lives and shape the ideas we have about ourselves? And, perhaps finally, what are its limits? After all, the world of private affairs is not our whole world – or is it?

Many argue that the world of private affairs can and should be the whole of our (social) world. They argue that the public dimension of our world ought to be as narrow as is consistent with making the private secure. Echoing Adam Smith, they argue that our government should limit itself to domestic and international security and to a few public works essential to economic intercourse but unlikely to be provided by private agents acting in their own interests.

What, then, are the limits of the world of private affairs? When must we have recourse to a public authority – government – because the private associations we create and the private transactions we engage in are either not enough or the wrong thing? When, moreover, is our self-interest a matter of public concern, and when can and should it be left entirely up to us?

Our answers to these questions depend on three broad considerations. First, they depend on how we judge self-interest, whether we consider it a virtue or a vice. The political economy I explore in this book does not consider self-interest a vice, although neither does it consider private ends the only ends. Second, the answers depend on how we understand our life together. Should it be limited, so far as possible, to private associations and transactions, or is more needed? How do our public and private lives interrelate? Finally, our answers to these questions depend on how we judge the functioning of the property system, especially the market. How does it work? When does it work well, and when does it not? What can it accomplish for us, and what must we accomplish in other ways?

These are questions for political economy. In the words of the greatest critic of political economy, Karl Marx, political economy studies the "anatomy of civil society." By civil society, Marx had in mind what I have referred to as the world of private affairs. Civil society is the system of human interactions ruled by self-interest and the use of private property to serve self-interest. This is the world of political economy, viewed always with an eye to its limits.

In order to explore this "anatomy of civil society," I develop some rudiments of a theory of market economy, one that I hope will be reasonably accurate and provide a foundation for answering some of the questions just posed. The theory I construct here highlights three interconnected themes of political economy, themes that focus the discussion of the limits of the world of private affairs: market economy as an engine of economic development, market economy as a foundation for liberty, and the problematic status of labor in market economy.

Adam Smith begins *The Wealth of Nations* with a theme regarding economic development, or the passage from the "savage state of man" to "civilized society." He begins by asking what differentiates these two states and how might we successfully pass from one to the other. This theme concerning development is taken up with considerable energy and brilliance by Karl Marx, who, while recasting the theme in his own language, continues to make it central to political economy. What makes some rich, others poor, some nations wealthy, others not? When political economy addresses these sorts of questions, it makes development its central theme. I have done so as well in the following.

Many refer to the goal of economic development as justification for the use of private property in the pursuit of private interest. Those who do often argue that the pursuit of private gain is the only motivation at all likely to bring about development from poverty to wealth. They justify the free market system on the grounds that unfettered pursuit of self-interest will bring prosperity by assuring the strongest possible link between contribution and remuneration.

The first theme concerning development leads the classical thinker naturally to the second concerning liberty. Liberty is both a theme and an argument. The argument claims to show how a certain kind of liberty, the liberty of commerce, will solve the problem of how we, individually and as a nation, make the passage from poverty to wealth. This peculiar sort of liberty frees us to own and use private property in labor and in means of production (or capital stock) to pursue our private ends. In this book I introduce some of the conceptual and analytical tools economists use to argue for and against free trade, the liberty of commerce, as a solution to the problem of economic development.

But the theme of liberty is not just about how we go from a savage state to a civilized society; it is also about why we might want to do so and what we might expect to accomplish. For the classical economist, development means the growth of wealth, and civilized society means wealthy society. Wealth bears heavily on our freedom. Wealth is important not simply because it assures that our basic needs will be met but also because a measure of wealth is necessary to assure our autonomy. In Chapter 2 I try to indicate why this might be the case. If it is, we can only be free in a wealthy society, which does not, of course, mean that if we happen to be in a wealthy society we must be free.

Liberty is, then, both means and end. But the liberty we think of as means is not clearly of the same order as the liberty we think of as end. The liberty we think of as means is the liberty of commerce – in short, free trade. It is the liberty of individuals, and corporations, to own the nation's capital stock as their private property and use it to their advantage. Private ownership of society's productive resources is the hallmark of the kind of liberty political economists have claimed will lead to economic development.

The liberty we think of as the end has more to do with individual self-determination, integrity, and responsibility. The theme centering on liberty speaks about our aspirations, individually and collectively, to assure the conditions needed to sustain our independence of action and initiative. Liberty has to do with the opportunities that society affords us to determine who we are and how we will lead our lives. Wealth allows us to develop and exercise our autonomy and individuality. With enough wealth to support our freedoms, we can take on the burden of responsibility for our lives. Political economy concerns itself with the framework of individual responsibility and its limits. Wealthy society provides opportunity and demands that the individual take responsibility for him- or her-self. Liberty links up with responsibility.

This link introduces our third theme. Capitalist economies treat the individual's capacities as commodities to be bought, sold and therefore valued in markets. The term labor market refers to the set of exchanges trading capacities for money. But not only are our capacities valued in markets and treated as commodities, their value in the market is the main determinant of our income and welfare. Because liberty depends on wealth and wealth on income, we must investigate the treatment of our capacities as commodities if we are to understand the implications of the market system for liberty.

The connection between the labor market and individual liberty, of course, goes beyond the way our access to wealth depends on the value of our capacities. Our ability to sell our labor for a wage or salary means that those capacities are ours in a special sense – they are our property. No other person or institution has the right to determine who we work for or what sort of work we do. This is also an important kind of liberty, although it is not without its hazards. When we have only the income from selling our capacities to live on, and when the market for those capacities is limited, our opportunities are limited. In many cases these limitations restrict our freedom more than they enhance it. Political economy can illuminate the complex relation between freedom and treating our capacities as commodities.

The treatment of labor as a commodity also has implications for the theme of development. The dependence of income on the sale of laboring capacity links income to production cost of which labor cost is a major component. The higher our wages and salaries, the higher our income; the higher our income, the more we can buy from those who hope to make a profit by selling things to us. At the same time the higher our wages and salaries, the more it costs those who hire us to help them produce those commodities. This means that the cost of labor has complex implications for the process of economic growth and development.

The connection of wealth to liberty makes wealth important and development worth the trouble. And trouble development most certainly is. The trouble arises because what we accomplish by development comes at a cost. This is also an important theme. Economic development is a social or national goal. It requires a vast mobilization of society in its service. Of those mobilized, only some, at times a small proportion, benefit much by it. The benefits become widespread only later. How we make development a goal matters.

The classical economists thought we could do so simply by setting individuals free to pursue their private interests as they perceived them. If we liberate commerce to pursue the goal of making the most money possible, then those engaged in commerce will do those things that lead to economic development. And, even though they appropriate a goodly share for their own personal use, they still devote a great deal of society's product, which they own as their private property, to building up capital stock for the future.

Many have doubted that economic development can be accomplished as the unintended consequence of private self-seeking, arguing instead that it must be made an explicit objective of government policy and that government must direct and regulate the economy so as to assure that resources are well used. I explore some dimensions of this debate in the following pages. The debate has to do with the limits of liberty, at least of the liberty of commerce. It has something to do as well with ends of government. These ends express how our nation understands its common or collective purpose, or in an older language, the public or common good.

Political economy has its own way of thinking about the public good, one that focuses attention on private ends. That is, political economists often think the public good consists of the sum of private goods. The public good refers, then, to what benefits each of us individually by enhancing our welfare through increasing our real income. This line of argument links the public good to the end of economic development, which enhances the ability of the economy to provide for the material well-being of citizens.

Public policy is often discussed with an eye to its consequences for the size or growth rate of the national product, the level of income, or the rate of employment. We judge policy by its impact on economic performance. This makes sense; but it is also in some ways limiting. Other criteria matter. The habit of judging public policy by economic performance shifts these other criteria into the background. Consider the example of education.

Concern over failing competitiveness and slow productivity growth leads some observers to advocate more government involvement. Thus more spending on education will, it is argued, improve our stock of educated labor capable of scientific discovery and application while raising the skill level and productivity of the work force. Government's education policy becomes a part of its economic policy. This makes impact on economic performance a measure of the success of social policy.

Defining problems in this way is consistent with making economic growth and development the objectives of public policy. Doing so opens up an important and valuable line of investigation. But, taken by itself, it leaves out a vital dimension and distorts our understanding of the role of government. The part left out has to do with considerations of social justice. Concern for social justice can guide economic policy in directions different from those that follow concern for economic performance.

Concern with social justice directs attention to the idea of individual opportunity. Development refers to the path toward social arrangements that assure to all persons, so far as possible, the array of opportunities needed for individual self-determination. Without employment and income, the individual's effort to realize his or her capacities must be seriously impaired. Thus economic policy aimed at economic objectives has its place. But the underlying justification for policy is not narrowly economic.

A better educated labor force may indeed be more productive (although it may also exhibit some qualities that work against productivity). But this does not make productivity the justification for government spending on education. A more compelling argument for investment in education holds regardless of its consequences for productivity. This argument links education to opportunity for individual self-determination.

Of course, if the point is to lobby for spending on education, why not appeal to a (perhaps dubious) relation between education and competitiveness if you think that argument might succeed? The result would seem to serve the cause of justice as well. But perhaps it does not. By employing economic arguments for social policy, we reinforce the idea that the role of government should be limited to making the market work better. This limitation can have damaging consequences. If it turns out that better schools will not enhance our productivity, the economic argument works against educational expenditure and thus against our concern for educational opportunity as a part of a movement toward greater social justice.

One way of expressing the difference between two ways of thinking about the role of government uses the language of rights and welfare (see Levine 1983a). Political economy carries on its arguments over policy in the language of welfare, loosely speaking of material well-being. This language is important, and concern over welfare is a legitimate end of political economy. But that concern needs to be carried forward into the context of a concern for individual rights and integrity. Concern for rights is not automatically met by improvements in welfare. Welfare and rights are not in fundamental conflict, but they are different. Each needs to be taken into account in a discussion of policy and the role of government.

Thinking this way connects two of the themes of political economy introduced earlier, those involving liberty and development. Placed within a context of concern for social justice, the expansion of freedom is the end of development. This makes policy in the interest of development subordinate to concern for justice, just as it makes justice the most powerful argument for development. In concern for social justice, we also have our most powerful argument for limiting the market and the process of economic development (i.e., when they threaten to damage justice and self-determination).

The considerations briefly introduced in this introduction suggest one other important dimension to debate in political economy. We normally link opportunity to equality by speaking of opportunity for all as "equal opportunity." Defining development as I have here must make concern over equality and inequality central. After exploring the core ideas of political economy concerning the workings of a market economy in Parts I and II, I turn to an investigation of the various arguments regarding equality and inequality.

I begin, in Part I, with an exploration of the idea of a self-standing economy and with the problem of the use of wealth. I attempt in this discussion to raise the core issues of political economy. In Part II I outline the basic features of a capitalist or private enterprise economy, which has been assumed by virtually all students to be the appropriate form of economic organization to assure the growth of wealth. This system exhibits a significant degree of inequality of income and wealth among citizens; and in Part III I consider the arguments advanced to justify inequality under capitalism. Part IV considers a set of related matters within a global setting, including questions of the role of the market, the roots of international inequality, and the emergence of global society. Part V considers arguments that justify setting limits on the free market and on the role of pursuit of private ends in organizing our social lives.

Economy and society

1

The place of the economy

The economy

We no longer know what to do with our economy. Will lowering taxes on the wealthy increase incomes and employment or simply enrich the wealthy? Do welfare programs and income supports assure well-being and meet our obligations to our fellow citizens? Or do they weaken the incentives to work and save, incentives that underpin prosperity?

Underlying such questions as these are broader uncertainties that motivate political debate and strain the social fabric, questions that have to do with the place of the economy in the larger social order. Does our economy work best when attended to least? Should management of economic affairs be more firmly attached to public ends and explicit strategies for achieving them?

Bill Clinton began his presidential campaign with a proclamation of faith:

We believe in the free enterprise system and the power of market forces. We know economic growth will be the best jobs program we will ever have. But economic growth does not come without a national economic strategy to invest in people and meet the competition. (Clinton & Gore 1992, p. 6)

Adam Smith, writing in 1776, also believed in the power of market forces and that encouraging economic growth was the best way of securing employment. But he did not share Clinton's conviction that a national economic strategy was needed to secure economic growth and prosperity.

The debate over the best means to secure the growth of wealth has raged more or less continuously for more than two hundred years. In reviewing this history it sometimes seems that our uncertainty about the economy is all uncertainty about means. But I do not think this is correct. Serious thought about ends is also needed. In the following I hope we can learn something about what troubles our economy by focusing on ends rather than means.

The uncertainty I refer to is not new. What to do with the economy has been a problem since we first became aware that we had one. Our awareness of the economy is, however, a fairly recent development.

Ancient societies engaged in what we might call economic activities. They produced and distributed the things needed to satisfy their members' wants. In doing so, they were sometimes more, sometimes less, successful, depending, for example, on the weather. Moving a step further back in history, primitive societies also went about trying with varying success to acquire what their members needed. Neither the ancients nor the primitives, however, spent much effort pondering what to do about their economies. Some did not even have a word for economy on which to focus their pondering. Even if they had some words they could use, they had no real reason to concern themselves with the recondite matters that now confuse us about economy. They did not have fiscal deficits, economic indicators, or economic policies.[1] They did not have economic doctrine because economic doctrine cannot "exist without the prior concept of 'the economy'" (Finley 1973, p. 155).

Another way to say this is to notice that premodern society did not separate the economy from the flow of daily life. It was not something distinct: a different place, a different way of doing things, or a different purpose for doing things. No one would have spoken then, as for example, Bill Clinton did in his 1993 State of the Union Address, about what troubles "our economy."

Late in the life of our society, perhaps as late as the eighteenth century, the economy became something to worry about. It was no longer just what most people did with their lives, it was an entity in its own right: a place we sometimes go, an activity we sometimes do, a thing we sometimes think about. I refer to this quality of the economy as its separateness.

Karl Polanyi was one of the first thinkers to concern himself explicitly with what I call the separateness of the economy.[2] He distinguishes between "embedded" and "disembedded" economies. The former are, so to speak, hidden in the fabric of society; the latter are a separate and notable realm exposed to conjecture, subject to thought and action.

The fabric in which the economy is originally embedded is the household. The anthropologist Marshall Sahlins notes that in primitive society, "the household makes up a kind of 'petite' economy." Here "the normal activities of any adult man, taken in conjunction with the normal activities of an adult

---

[1] M. I. Finley observes that the work, Xenophon's *Oikonomikos*, which became the model for a 2000 year tradition of writing on economics, contains "not one sentence that expresses an economic principle or offers any economic analysis, nothing on efficiency of production, 'rational' choice, the marketing of crops" (1973, p. 19).

[2] See Polanyi (1957). The first to explore this idea systematically was the German philosopher G.W.F. Hegel in his *Philosophy of Right*.

woman, practically exhaust the customry works of society" (1972, pp. 78–79).

Sahlins's description of the household economy bears little resemblance to the world we live in. We can hardly imagine satisfying our wants if all we can call on is the work and know-how of ourselves, our spouse, and perhaps a child or two. Embedding the economy in the household, then, means radically limiting what we can want and what we can get to satisfy our wants.

It also means isolating ourselves from the larger world. Sahlins goes on to observe that the social economy of primitive society "is fragmented into a thousand petty existences, each organized to proceed independently of the others and each dedicated to the homebred principle of looking out for itself" (1972, p. 95).

This observation brings us to one of the most salient features of our own "disembedded" economy. Members of household economies depend on their relatives to help in acquiring the things needed for daily life. They have a close relation to a limited group of others responsible for securing the family's survival. Today, we depend on those we have no close relations with, people we do not know, strangers rather than relatives.

The term political economy was introduced in the eighteenth century to distinguish the new boundaries of economic life: "What oeconomy is in a family, political economy is in a state" (Steuart 1966/1767, p. 16). Reference to political economy puts us on notice that economic affairs take place among strangers rather than relatives.

We do not produce the things we consume; they come from other regions and nations: cars from Germany, Japan, or Korea, sweaters from Italy, shirts from Singapore, smoked oysters from Thailand, cheese from France or Britain, beer from Australia. They are produced by people we do not know. Aside from buying their products, we may have little relation with them. If they are fellow citizens, we share that much common life; if they are not, buying and selling may be virtually the whole of our connection.

Yet, in buying their produce, we enter into a significant relation with them. Not only do money and goods circulate but also ways of life. We have access to different cultures, and we can, in however limited a way, participate in them by feeling their influence in the things we use. We are more separate from those we depend on because we do not know them, but we are also better connected because we come to share more of our lives with them. We lose some of the isolation of the household economy.

Considered on the global level, the United States has felt this loss of isolation less powerfully because of the special influence American culture has had worldwide. Wherever we are in the world, we can eat at McDonalds, watch American television shows, drive American cars. Part of the reason for this is the dominance of the U.S. market. Its size makes it profitable for producers abroad to adapt to it rather than attempt to adapt it to the kinds of goods they might produce for their own citizens. A second reason is the political and cultural influence of the United States across the globe. This influence has made a disproportionate amount of global culture American culture. As a result we have benefited less from exposure to other cultures than they have from exposure to ours. The world market opens all participants to a marketplace of cultures, but it has done so asymmetrically. As the global predominance of the United States wanes, this asymmetry should weaken and our culture should open up to influences from around the world.

Clearly, our economy is no longer synonymous with our daily routine. The members of the household were their economy, the daily life of the household its economic activities. For us, by contrast, though we may buy, sell, and work, our economy exists with or without us. It is separate from us. In Polanyi's language, the economy is now disembedded.

Because the economy is disembedded, we need to think about what to do with it. Thinking what to do about the economy spawned the discipline of political economy in the eighteenth century. One of the founders of political economy, Sir James Steuart, describes it this way:

The principal object of this science is to secure a certain fund of subsistence for all the inhabitants, to obviate every circumstance which may render it precarious; to provide everything necessary for supplying the wants of society, and to employ the inhabitants (supposing them to be free men) in such a manner as naturally to create reciprocal relations and dependencies between them, so as to make their several interests lead them to supply one another with their reciprocal wants. (1966/1767, p. 17)

Steuart believes that in order to satisfy wants, we will need to know a science. Evidently, the economy is a thing we do not know as much about as we need to if we are to prosper. If economy consisted of a man and woman producing their subsistence, this knowledge would hardly be necessary.

The question of control becomes important when the economy is disembedded. The members of the household economy had a kind of control, although forces of nature could easily overwhelm what control they had. But they did not have an economy to control. Economy was the stuff of their lives; it was what they did. It was not something to control. Perhaps the male head of the household ran the show in the primitive economy. But, if he did control others, this does not mean that controlling the economy was his concern.

Concern about control goes together with the prospect that something might get out of control. This is a concern that comes our way with the emergence of the economy. Our dependence is no longer simply on ourselves but also on others and on "the economy."

Our welfare depends on the price of oil, which depends on decisions made by strangers. But even that observation misses the main point. Our welfare depends not only on the decisions of strangers but also on the workings of the thing we call the economy. What the economy does to and for us depends on decisions others make, but it is not decided by them. All those decisions to buy and sell, save and invest, work and not work, add up in ways unintended and unpredictable.

We may talk about our economy in the way we talk about our cars. When something goes wrong with our car, we need to get it fixed because we depend on it. But we do not need to change ourselves to fix our cars. Or we may talk about our economies in the way we talk about our bodies. Sometimes we can get our bodies fixed without changing ourselves, but sometimes we cannot. Sometimes getting along with our bodies means changing ourselves.

If a disease or accident takes away our ability to walk, dealing with that change in our body demands some change in ourselves. We must see ourselves in a wheelchair rather than walking, and this can change our perspective on the world and our place in it. As we age, changes in our bodies demand that we change our images of ourselves and the way we live. We may continue to have an image of ourselves as young long after we have turned the corner into middle age. This false self-image can get us into trouble, leading us to attempt things we cannot do or behave in ways not appropriate for us. We may sense that something is wrong. To fix what is wrong we must change the way we see ourselves.

Is our relationship to our economy like that to our car or like that to our body? When our economy fails to work right, does this imply that something is wrong with the way we lead our lives or imagine ourselves?

Economists have come to think about the economy mainly as though it were like a car. They believe their expertise gives them the skill to fix it without significantly touching the lives of those who use and depend on it. Of course, fixing our economy will make our lives better, but it does not make us different. Many critics dispute this judgment. They believe we cannot fix the economy without changing ourselves, although there is not much agreement on the changes needed.

Many today think we need to be more self-denying. We need to make sacrifices, get less, save more. We cannot continue to be the people we have been if the economy is to work well. Ross Perot drew support with this sentiment during the 1992 presidential election campaign. The winning candidate and his other opponent reassured the electorate that they need not change themselves to fix their economy. They believed the economy was more like our car than our body.

Laissez-faire

Sir James Steuart, writing at the end of the eighteenth century, thought the economy would only work well if someone took responsibility for it. Steuart refers to this someone as the "statesman." Adam Smith, often considered the founder of political economy, saw things differently. In his great work *The Wealth of Nations*, published in 1776, Smith argued that the economy would work well if it were left alone, thus the doctrine of laissez-faire.

By the time Smith wrote his treatise on political economy, much of economic life was organized through markets rather than through a household division of labor. The economy was a system of activities connected by purchase and sale of goods and labor. How we satisfy our wants and the kinds of wants we have to satisfy depend on the market and our relation to it.

The doctrine of laissez-faire implied a particularly radical separation of the economy. Not only was it no longer a part of the household, subsumed into the daily life of a small, more or less self-sufficient, group, but it was now a world of its own, expected to look after itself. The political institutions, or public authority, need not take over from the head of the household responsibility for seeing to it that the means for satisfying wants are produced and distributed. The free, or self-regulating, market stands apart from politics and government as much as it does from the household and its head. This economy is truly disembedded.

One of the most striking features of the laissez-faire market economy is that in it, as C. E. Lindblom observes, "livelihood is at stake in exchange" (1977, p. 47). What we own and its price determine what we can buy. Because virtually all the things we need must be bought from others, the price of what we own determines what needs, if any, we can satisfy.

The doctrine of laissez-faire carries the implication that we do not need the interventions of the statesman to assure that our wants will be satisfied. That doctrine asserts that the market will, on its own, offer us a price for what we own adequate for us to buy the things we need at the prices the market demands for them.

Assume, for example, that the only property you own that has any value is your ability to work – your laboring capacity. Assume also that the value of your ability to work is set by market forces depending, among other things, on how much interest there is in using your working capacity (demand for your labor). Perhaps only cheap restaurants are interested in buying your labor, and its price depends on how much they are willing and able to pay you. If the market sets the price of your labor at $5 per hour and you work 40 hours per week, then your weekly income is $200. From your standpoint, the market works well enough if you can acquire the things you need each week for no more than $200. This means that the prices of those things – the rent for your apartment, the prices of groceries, the costs of fuel and upkeep for your car, of clothes, of utilities – must add up to no more than $200.

The market might set the price of your labor too low for you to buy the things you need at the prices demanded for them. The poor fail to get a price for their labor adequate to enable them to buy what they need. Minimum wage laws embody the idea that there is a price below which labor should not be bought and sold. Such legislation expresses our doubt that welfare is assured when welfare depends on exchange.

Getting wages and prices in the right relation becomes the task of the market in a society that makes livelihood depend on exchange. Such a society makes the economy a separate system and expects that system to operate reasonably well on its own, without public control or direction. The market fails when, for example, the price of oil becomes so high relative to the average income of consumers that they cannot afford to buy it and thus cannot heat their houses, or cannot buy it without giving up other things they need such as trips to the doctor, regular meals, or decent clothes.

From the time of Adam Smith, the greatest energies of the science that has come to be called economics were devoted to finding out how and how well a freestanding market system would succeed in satisfying wants. Would those forces natural to markets establish prices of and demand for goods and labor appropriate to feed the workers and renew the means of production, securing the maintenance of the group? If the market does this, wants will be satisfied. But wants were satisfied by the household economy without the market. Or were they? Adam Smith describes primitive societies as "so miserably poor, that from mere want, they are frequently reduced, to the necessity sometimes of directly destroying, and sometimes of abandoning their infants, their old people, and those afflicted with lingering diseases, to perish with hunger or to be devoured by wild beasts" (1937/1776, p. lviii). However true in isolated cases, Smith's characterization of life in the early stages of society is more myth than history. Anthropological evidence does not support the idea that primitive economy was a system of deprivation. Sahlins reports results of ethnographic studies showing that for some primitive societies, the "food quest is so successful that half the time the people seem not to know what to do with themselves" (1972, p. 11).

Depending on their particular geographic setting and circumstances, the early tribes got along well enough. If this is so, then what do we gain by making livelihood depend on exchange? And in order to gain this reward, do we need a statesman to oversee the market and make sure it provides what we need to satisfy our wants? What is the place of economy in the larger fabric of our lives together?

The use of markets

What are markets for? Adam Smith's answer centered on the accumulation of wealth. We have markets to enable us individually and as a society to become wealthy, not just to satisfy the limited wants of our primitive ancestors but to satisfy the wants of what he termed "civilized society."

The primitive tribes whose food quest was so successful that they did not know what to do with themselves did not have malls to visit, televisions to watch, cars to take trips in, or computers to write books on. They may have satisfied their wants but, compared to us, they didn't want much.

The classical economists of the late eighteenth and early nineteenth centuries,[3] who first fully took notice of "the economy" and studied it as if it were a thing apart, also believed that our wants are without limit. David Ricardo, writing in 1817, quotes Adam Smith's observation "that the desire for food is limited in every man by the narrow capacity of the human stomach, but the desire of the conveniences and ornaments of building, dress, equipage, and household furniture, seems to have no limit or certain boundary." For Ricardo, as for economists to this day, "to procure these gratifications in the greatest abundance is the object in view" (1951/1817, p. 293).

We have markets, then, not to assure that our meager wants get satisfied but to provide us that something more than the bare necessities that makes life civilized: luxury, riches, wealth. By the time the classical economists came along, life was considerably more "civilized," at least for some, than it was for members of those tribes who could not figure out what to do with themselves once they had enough food to go around. As we do now, the early economists took it for granted that becoming civilized was a good idea.

Looking backward, few of us find the simple life of the early humans very enticing. We do not want to give up our "luxuries," which, through use, have become more like necessities. Because of this, we look upon our early ancestors as we might look on today's homeless. We think them deprived. But, lacking benefit of the modern perspective, they felt neither deprived nor impoverished. If Sahlins is correct, they did have a great deal of leisure time and lived their own sort of "primitive affluence."

Early humans did not spend much time writing books, pleading cases in court, planning corporate takeovers, repairing cars, mowing lawns, or learning foreign languages. They were neither poor nor wealthy, but they got along.

The disembedded economy is meant to bring us wealth and turn our society into a wealthy society, to bring about the transition, as Adam Smith describes it, from the savage state of man to civilized society. Karl Marx

---

[3] For further discussion of the Classical school in economics, see Dobb (1973), Levine (1977), and Walsh and Gram (1980).

(1848) repeats Smith's judgment, seeing in the modern market system a great engine of progress that creates the foundation for abundance in a world society. But if humans got along well enough without wealth, why work so hard and go to so much trouble to get it? We would not need people writing books about "the economy" if we took our economic activities for granted, if experiencing them was enough, thinking about them beside the point.

These considerations lead me to two questions: Why are market economies specially suited to encouraging the growth of wealth? And what do we need wealth for? The first question has been the stuff of economics for the past three hundred years. In Part II I summarize some of our thinking on this issue. But my main purpose is to explore the answer to the second question. It has received less attention than the first, but it is not less important. To justify separating the economy within the larger set of social institutions, it is not enough to assert, or even demonstrate, that a self-standing market brings about the growth of wealth. We also need to know what we want wealth for. We need to know this not because it might reinforce our commitment, if any, to the system – capitalism – that brings about the expansion of wealth but because we need to know when we have enough and when our quest for wealth might end.

2

Needs and wants

The multiplication of wants

Our early ancestors differed from us not primarily in whether their wants were satisfied but in the kinds of wants they had. We want more than they did, and we want differently. Our wants develop in many directions and change continually. Wants multiply with the multiplication of the means to satisfy them. By contrast, the consumption habits, and thus the wants, of early humans did not change much. Why this multiplication of wants and of means in modern society (Hegel 1951, pp. 122–29)? I think three interconnected objectives go a long way in accounting for modern man's desire for wealth. They are esteem, autonomy, and security.

Esteem

"The possession of wealth confers honor" as the American economist and sociologist Thorstein Veblen observed (1899, p. 26). Desire for the regard of others looms large in any explanation of the desire for wealth. It plays its part in primitive societies where the little wealth available could still be used to establish differences in status between those that have some or more and those that have none or less. This use of wealth is exemplified by the potlatch of Native American peoples of the Pacific Northwest:

"Potlatching" is the giving away of food and wealth in return for recognition of the giver's social status. The more that is given away, the higher the status. (Adams 1973, p. 1)

The wealth given away in the potlatch represents, and thus measures, the "true worth" of the giver.

The connection between wealth and worth has different forms in different historical settings. What is curious about the potlatch is that it is the giving away rather than the amassing of wealth that determines status. But, of course, to give it away, you must first amass it. So the need to use wealth to establish status by giving away wealth demands that we first devote ourselves to accumulation. The potlatch solves a problem posed by wealth accumulation: what to do with it. It simply solves it differently than we do today.

Destroying wealth also gives evidence of wealthiness, as you cannot destroy what you do not have. Among the Kwakiutl, the central symbol of wealth, power, and prestige was the copper, "a shield shaped plate of beaten copper that usually has a painted or engraved representation of a crest animal on its surface" (Jonaitis 1991, p. 12). Referring to this symbol, Jonaitis notes:

A chief might break a copper, destroying the integrity of the crest design. He would then offer the broken pieces to his rival, who then had to break a copper of equal or higher value. A rival unable to do so would be humiliated before the community. (p. 40)

Destruction of wealth, in its way, anticipates what Veblen refers to as "conspicuous waste." The example suggests what a long tradition stands behind the commonplace notion that the ability to make waste determines social status.

The desire for wealth is the desire to mark out a social position. Different groups in society live differently. The amount of wealth needed depends on the group to which one belongs. An aristocrat needs more than a peasant because leading the life of an aristocrat is more expensive than leading the life of a peasant. To be recognizable as an aristocrat, you must dress in aristocratic clothes, eat the appropriate food, live in the appropriate accommodations. This is true in different contexts:

In Aztec society rank was displayed by the wearing of feathers on the head and on the robes, as well as by bright colors and the wearing of gold and jewels. The ordinary ranks wore only a loincloth, and the women a simple cotton dress down to the ankles. (de Marly 1990, p. 9)

In ancient Egypt only those in high position could wear sandals; the Greeks and Romans controlled type, color and number of garments worn and the sorts of embroidery with which they could be trimmed. (Lurie 1981, p. 115)

As class barriers erode, cost of materials becomes the benchmark of status: "rich materials, superfluous trimmings and difficult-to-care-for styles." Another way to establish status via dress is through amount, "to wear more clothes than other people do" is an example of what Lurie terms "conspicuous multiplication" (p. 120).

To be an aristocrat, of course, dress is not enough. One must also have the "bearing" of an aristocrat. But the only way to get an aristocratic bearing is to live among aristocrats, which only those with adequate wealth can afford. Wealth, of course, may not be enough. Birth and connections also count heavily. But the less wealth that comes one's way, the more tenuous one's attachment to the aristocracy will be.

Aristocrats need more because having more maintains membership in the aristocracy. If we are to organize our society into aristocrats and peasants, we must distribute wealth accordingly.

The classical economists incorporated this idea about the use of wealth into their accounts of market society. They distinguished between those who got by on the "subsistence" and those who required luxuries and wealth to maintain the style of life appropriate to their class. Thus wealth was used to establish class position. Those with little or no wealth belonged to the laboring class. Their needs were met not by wealth, but by subsistence.[1]

The term subsistence connotes the means to satisfy basic human needs. Sometimes such needs are linked to physiological requirements of life. When shelter and clothing are just to protect us from the elements, food to fend off starvation, then they are part of the bare subsistence in the physiological sense.

But society does not remain long at this level and also remain *human* society. To be human, we must satisfy our needs in a human sort of way. This means that even subsistence includes things required to maintain a minimal but still human way of life. Perhaps we could survive within a herdlike existence where we all wore the same clothing and ate the most basic of foods (the kind of feed we provide cattle, but nutritionally appropriate to our species). Even if we could (and that is far from certain), we would not survive in our human condition. Even subsistence contains an element aimed at establishing regard for our humanness.

Veblen placed the pursuit of esteem at the center of his analysis of wealthy societies. For Veblen, the dominant incentive for the acquisition of wealth "was the invidious distinction attaching to wealth" (1899, p. 26). In this context, wealth is used to create a hierarchy of esteem in which some are better than others.

Markets play an important part in enabling and encouraging us to use wealth in this way. They do so by providing us with a measure of our worth as persons. Markets place a value (or price) on goods used to satisfy wants. In the market, the measure of a good is the amount of money it can command, not the need it can satisfy. The market measures bread in dollars (or yen or marks) rather than in loaves (see Levine 1983b).

Money rather than want satisfaction is the measure of wealth; indeed, money is the unit of wealth. The money measure allows us to want wealth for its own sake, that is, to want an amount of wealth as much as we want the things wealth consists of.

Thus markets provide us with a quantitative measure of our worth as persons: the amount of wealth we own. By making our wealth a measure of

---

[1] For further discussion, see *Journal of Income Distribution* (1992).

our worth, society makes the pursuit of wealth for its own sake a compelling goal. Of course, this goal motivates some more than others. Indeed, a normal prerequisite to becoming wealthy is wanting to become wealthy. Many do not desire wealth. Not all who desire wealth acquire it, and not all who lack interest in wealth remain poor. Yet, a desire to be wealthy leads some to devote their lives to the pursuit of wealth.

Invidious comparison undermines equality. Members of minority groups who face constricted opportunities due to unemployment or inferior education may not simply feel poorer than the affluent suburbanite; they may also feel that they bear an inferior status. They may be treated and regarded as lesser citizens, or not as citizens at all. Civil unrest in urban areas has much to do with the tension between the idea of equality of persons and the experience of inferiority that results in part from inequalities of wealth and opportunity.

This means that a society made wealthy by encouraging the pursuit of wealthiness as an end in itself entails a dilemma. Can we be equal as persons while having vastly unequal access to the wealth that defines the opportunities available to persons? The argument for private enterprise assumes that inequality of wealth does not challenge the basic equality of persons. But, it might; and civil unrest, when linked to poverty and restricted opportunity, warns us of the hazards of too easily assuming that we can be treated equally as persons when our life chances differ so dramatically.

In market societies there are always some, the "poor," who have little or no wealth. But in the nineteenth century, members of the laboring classes had little or no wealth, and perhaps were all poor if poor means being without the wealth needed to elicit the regard of others (see Polanyi 1957). Now, in the industrialized countries, poverty is primarily the plight of those who cannot find work.[2] If, then, the laboring classes are not poor, they must have a measure of wealth. Even if ownership and nonownership of wealth does not distinguish classes, amount of wealth can. And even if we overlook class differences, differences in amount of wealth can mean differences in social status and in the regard of others.

This raises an important question. As we have seen, wealth is connected to differences between persons. Historically, these differences are differences in social status, which could affect not only social position but also self-esteem. Thus historically, the differences between persons linked to ownership of wealth meant inequality of persons who occupied different positions in a hierarchy. Thus the question: Does the use of wealth to establish differences in ways of life between persons imply its use to create in-

---

[2] As we will see, this is only accurate up to a point because many who work are poor. But in the industrialized world, most of those who work are not poor, whereas in the nonindustrialized world, work is less of a protection against poverty. See Chapter 7.

equality in status and esteem? I explore the relation between difference and inequality further in Part III.

The esteem we have for others need not vary with their wealth. If it does not, then it is possible that we all need some wealth to lead our lives and escape from poverty; but we do not need an ever growing amount of wealth to enhance our social position. Tying esteem to wealth creates a measure of esteem appropriate for ranking persons. It means that the more wealth we have the greater our regard in the eyes of others and therefore possibly in our own. And this gives us a powerful motive to try to acquire as much wealth as we can. The pursuit of ever larger accumulations of wealth follows from the link between wealth and esteem, which, then, helps explain the value we place on wealth expansion.

Autonomy

In a market society, individuals take responsibility for satisfying their wants. They must know what they want and how to go about acquiring the things that will satisfy those wants. Wants differ for different persons. What we want is closely linked to who we are and hope to be. The things we consume help to define our way of life, which, in turn, expresses our sense of self: the idea we have of who we are or might become. Wealth can provide us the opportunity to make our wants and our ways of life peculiarly our own. Wealth expands and changes the opportunities available to us.

In premodern societies, such opportunities existed only to a very limited degree (see Sahlins 1972, Chapter 1). Ways of life and modes of consumption varied little from member to member (within classes or status groups). In premodern society, the group we belonged to rather than who we were individually determined our way of life. Aristocrats and peasants, men and women, slave owner and slave defined groups whose lives differed significantly. Within those groups, however, individuality was less essential. The purpose of a way of life was to establish status in the eyes of others, and this depended on establishing by dress and demeanor our group membership. The shared ways of life of the premodern culture contrast with the individualized ways of life of participants in a modern market society. Concepts such as self-determination, individual freedom, and choice take on greater importance and add a vital dimension to the way we decide what to produce and consume.

The market can play a significant role in allowing, encouraging, even requiring individuals to make decisions for themselves, choose among alternatives according to criteria arising from within, and take responsibility for the consequences of their decisions. But it is not always easy to know when decisions come from within and when they do not, when people want what they want and when they only "think that they want or are interested in what actually they only believe they should want or be interested in" (Shapiro 1981, p. 26).

Toward the end of the nineteenth century, economists developed a peculiar way of thinking about wants that made the issue of their origin considerably less troublesome. They, in effect, assumed that people know what they want, want what they want, and gain satisfaction from consuming the things they want. This idea encouraged a kind of celebration of the market (see Friedman 1962, and Hayek 1945). Markets enable those with the means to decide for themselves what they will acquire to satisfy their wants. Freedom became synonymous with choice. Markets were advanced as institutions that assure choice.

Two propositions capture the link among freedom, markets, and choice: (1) markets make choices available, and (2) markets enable buyers to choose. Choice sometimes refers to the availability of alternatives, sometimes to the activity of deciding among alternatives. In describing the emergence of the supermarket, one student sketched a familiar picture that highlights the complex relation between the two aspects of choice:

> Long rows of canned, bottled, or packaged foods were offered in bright, warm colors, with striking or catchy names to stimulate sales. A chain store in a year might drop a thousand items, add more, and carry ten thousand or so in all. At times these foods changed in appearance, cost, or nutritive value, making an intelligent choice among them difficult. (Hooker 1981, p. 349)

Markets often provide choices in the sense of alternatives among which I can choose.[3] But having alternatives available and having the outcome in my hands also mean that I have to make a choice. The existence of options does not by itself enable me to choose. I must also be free from coercion by others and have the resources necessary to buy what I want. I must have the ability to decide among options. In other words, I must have the legal standing, the material means, the appropriate knowledge and information, and the psychic resources needed to choose.

By material means, I have in mind the money required to pay the price. The link between choice and freedom thus implies a link between freedom and wealth. If I have too little wealth, then I have few if any choices. The market only offers choices to those with the means to pay. By legal standing, I mean the recognized status of a property owner and independent agent. By knowledge, I mean appropriate and accurate information in a form I can understand. By psychic resources, I mean the capacity to know what I want and to act on that knowledge. Even if I have the legal standing, I might fall

---

[3] They do not always do so. Competition between a large number of sellers often leads to market structures – oligopoly and monopoly – that limit consumers' options.

short in capacity and ability, in which case I cannot choose, regardless of whether the market makes choice available to me.

Legally, the capacity to choose is linked to the right to own property and enter into contracts. The market is a system of legally voluntary contracts. This means that each party is legally free to buy what is offered or pass it up for something else or nothing at all. The legal status conferred by society on adults protects them from being coerced to buy or sell against their will. Making the contract an act of will in the legal sense makes it a freely undertaken decision, a kind of choice. Because markets consist of voluntary contracts between property owners, they incorporate the status that implies the legal capacity to choose.

Sometimes we assume that protection of our legal right to enter into a contract or refrain from doing so assures us the capacity to choose, that legal recognition of our capacity to be the agents of our actions implies that we do, indeed, act on our will, that what we get is what we want and that what we want springs from within. If this were so, then a market society would clearly assure freedom for those who have the requisite means (wealth).

But even in a market society those with the material means may find choosing a daunting task. It does, after all, require us to know what we want. Here the economist's assumption about wanting gets in the way. Economists, because they assume that people know what they want, can go on to connect markets directly to choice and freedom to markets. This makes the market the source of freedom, rather than one institution capable, in certain circumstances, of supporting freedom. What gets in the way of our knowing what we want and places us in situations where we find we do not want what we thought we did?

Obviously misleading information about goods can result in dissatisfaction from consuming them. If I am led to believe that a weight loss program will change my life, I may think it gives me what I want when it likely does not. Advertising often promotes products on grounds bearing at best a limited relation to what those products can actually provide. When advertising works this way, it contributes to the gap between what we think we want and what we really want. Some other examples suggest deeper reasons why such a gap might arise.

If I need surgery to repair a damaged knee, surgery may alleviate my pain and enable me (eventually) to lead an active life once again. I want what I think I want and getting what I want will likely satisfy my need. But I may want surgery to straighten or shorten a nose I feel is unsightly and the reason why my social and professional lives have failed. Getting what I want in this case is likely to leave me unsatisfied. Or, put the other way, it may turn out that I do not really want what I think I want.

I may want to win a prize in my field because doing so brings recognition, honor, and respect. Gaining honor may enhance my self-esteem and provide me with a good feeling about myself. To the extent that it does, getting what I want satisfies me. But it may not. Gaining honor may simply feed a bottomless craving for the respect and notice of others, a craving that no honor can satisfy because the others whose regard I seek are not the ones whose notice I really need. Ignored by my parents at an early age, or eclipsed by my siblings, what I really want is for my parents to take notice or for my siblings to be removed so that I can be the center of life in my family. I think I want the regard of my peers, but I really want my mother's love or my father's admiration. Getting the former does not gain me the latter. Getting what I think I want does not get me what I want; it leaves me unsatisfied.

Perhaps I want to attend medical school because my parents need me to be a doctor or because, among my peers, going to medical school is the right or the most highly regarded thing to do. If so, what I want is what I think I ought to want. I may still think I want it, but sooner or later I am likely to find myself unsatisfied no matter how successful I am in my medical career. This will happen if being a doctor does not really suit me, if I have the soul of an artist or of a farmer.

Sometimes we do not know why we want what we want. Is it the desire of others that drives what we want? Is it a sense of duty? Is it an emptiness of spirit, a longing for recognition that nothing we want could really satisfy?

Difficulties in wanting and especially in connecting want to satisfaction arise because what we want involves a relationship with others and an idea about ourselves. We want self-esteem and the esteem of others that we hope will be forthcoming if we get the things we think we want. Problems arise, in other words, because when we want particular things – an operation, an award, a career – what we really want is a relation with others and place in the world. This is the relational element in wanting.

If the relational element causes the trouble, it does so in league with another dimension: the thoughtful element in wanting. When we want something, we imagine a relation with another person or with an important group that might be realized through acquiring it. We imagine ourselves in relation to persons and things. This is what I mean by the thoughtful element in wanting: the anticipation in thought of a satisfying reality.

What we anticipate is the living out in reality of an idea we have of ourselves. This "ideal self" (Joffe and Sandler 1987; Chasseguet-Smirgel 1985) motivates us to act in the world. It is what we want; it is the reason we want; and it defines the particular things we want.

I want a membership in a health club because it will enable me to shape my body according to an ideal image (perhaps evoked for me by the ideal bodies reproduced in the health club's advertising campaign). By attaining this ideal, I believe I will satisfy myself. I also imagine that I will gain the

esteem of others and facilitate relationships with them more in tune with my
ideal self. Membership in the health club connects to romantic hopes and
career ambitions.

But the ideal self I strive for may or may not be my own. If it is not, then
the closer I come to attaining it, the farther I will be from myself. The more
closely I mold my body to the image in the poster, the less I see myself in it.
After all, I am molding my body after the image of another, and I may be
doing so in order to attain the admiration of others. But the admiration of
others I attain will really be for another, the other of an alien image.

Choosing means deciding which of the accessible options will best realize
our ideal, and thus suit us. Choosing is matching things in the world with
our subjective sense of our place in that world. Choosing requires us to think
about ourselves, to imagine ourselves in different places, and to know
enough about ourselves to judge who we are and therefore what we want.

Choosing goes awry when we do not know ourselves well, or when we
aspire to conflicting ideals. Then our choice is unlikely to yield the satisfaction that can only come from a good enough match between ourselves and
the things we surround ourselves with.

Some people do not think they make choices, and do everything they can
to avoid choice. They will go to dinner wherever their companions wish to
go. They respond to the question what do you want for dinner by saying
"whatever you want." They buy the clothes the salesperson tells them are
best, the house toward which their real estate agent directs them. They
pursue the careers their parents want them to pursue. They may face options and end up with one among the possible alternatives, but they do not
choose.

The life they find for themselves is one that others have found for them.
They are unlikely to find satisfaction because their aim is to satisfy others.
They do not know what they want because what they want depends on what
others want; in effect, they do not want. And if they seem to want things, this
does not mean that satisfaction will result from their getting those things.

Failure in the capacity to choose is a failure of autonomy. Strictly speaking, failure of autonomy means a failure to be your own person. Being
someone else's person means wanting what you think the other wants. This
does not happen primarily because others force us to do their bidding. It
happens because we cannot find ourselves and our own needs, or if we do,
we falter because we feel that acting places us in danger – for example, the
danger that we might lose the regard or affection of others. Autonomy is the
sense of having an inner core capable of identifying wants and pursuing their
satisfaction (Kohut 1977; Winnicott 1965). It enables us to choose and thus
take advantage of the opportunities made available by the presence of alternatives and by the legal standing associated with property ownership.

To be autonomous, we must have a place for ourselves. We need some wealth to form a place of our own, to form, in the words of one student, "the discrete living villages (composed of all those objects we select to cultivate our needs, wishes, and interests) that we create during our lifetime" (Bollas 1989, p. 9). The use of wealth to form a place of our own makes a measure of wealth necessary for autonomy. It connects wealth to privacy and privacy to freedom.

The institutions of private property gain significance because of the way they secure our "living villages." Private property protects the terrain of the self. It prevents others from entering that terrain other than by invitation. If the creation of a world for ourselves is our purpose in owning property, then this tells us something important about the kinds of things that are suitable for private ownership and thus for market exchange. I return to this connection in Chapter 14.

Security

Autonomy thrives in an atmosphere of safety (Joffe and Sandler 1987; Shafer 1983). We can only be autonomous when it is safe for us to know and be ourselves. For us to be safe in this sense requires that many conditions be met. In working to meet these conditions, wealth is often useful and sometimes vital. Wealth can increase security in several ways. One of the oldest of these is the use of wealth as saved-up sustenance: means of life over and above what is needed when times are good, stored up against the prospect that times will not always be so good. The more wealth we have to stand against hard times, the greater our security.

But wealth has more to contribute to security than its ability to feed people when the hunt and the harvest fail. Wealth supports specialization, allowing us to devote a part of the population to developing science and technology, which foster life-sustaining and life-supporting knowledge. Members of wealthy societies live longer and live in better repair than do members of societies with little wealth (see Table 11.1).[4] Society uses part of its wealth to buy longevity and physical well-being, both of which enhance security.

Scientific knowledge can also lower the risk that the harvest will, indeed, fail by increasing the yield of agriculture, securing crops against at least some of the hazards that might otherwise destroy them, fostering diversity that protects against failures in individual crops, facilitating the transportation of the means of life across long distances.

---

[4] Wealth can also endanger life. We all know many examples of ill health resulting from a wealthy lifestyle.

As I mentioned in Chapter 1, the disembedded economy links strangers across great distances in a system of mutual dependence. This makes us dependent on people we do not know, unlike the household economy which made us dependent primarily on our other family members. This growing circle of dependence can increase our security. The larger the system we have to depend on, the less we are subject to the vagaries of individual fate.

Thus, at least potentially, the change in our system of dependence can increase our security. However, it does not always do so (see Part II). Indeed, that we now depend on the economy and not on particular persons we know well can make us less secure if the economy works poorly, as it often does. Still, the potential for wealth to make us more secure remains and feeds one of the deepest motivations we have to pursue wealth and attempt to transform our societies into wealthy societies.

Needs and wants

The link between markets and choice provides a basis for linking markets to autonomy. But this connection has its limits. Understanding these limits is vital to determining the limits of the market and the role of government in satisfying needs. A distinction that proves helpful in thinking about the limits of the market and the role of government separates needs into two categories: those for which individual choice plays a primary role and those for which it does not. In the following, I refer to the first type as wants and the second as needs.

When I become sick, I need medical attention. Although an element of choice may enter (concerning, for example, the attitude or gender I prefer in a doctor), medical care is not essentially a matter of choice. And, indeed, the more urgent the problem (the more urgent my need), the smaller the role of choice. Heating my house has a similar quality. I may be concerned with cost (and possibly with environmental impact), but ultimately heat is heat; I simply need to be warm enough to go about the business of life.

The debate over national health insurance highlights issues of need and choice. We employ the market to distribute care in order to assure choice. In the case of medical care, there is not one issue of choice, there are two. The first has to do with participation of the patient in the process of determining care. The second has to do with how the quality of care is determined. Consumers might choose to spend more or less on health care. To see the implications of these two kinds of choice, consider some options for health care provision.

One can imagine a nationalized system that allocates care (including doctors). Citizens are the passive recipients of care. They do not choose their doctors or decide among possible treatment options. They do not choose how much to spend on care. A system such as this makes neither kind of choice available to the consumer.

A second system provides governmentally funded health insurance covering all citizens. The government funds and regulates insurance (or provides the insurance itself) in order to assure that all have equal coverage. But individuals can use their coverage in different ways, by choosing their doctors according to their ideas about health care: the relation of body to mind, the significance of prevention, and so on. In this case, the market plays a role because the doctor-patient relation includes a contract between the two. Such systems offer the first but not the second kind of choice.

A third system offers governmentally subsidized health insurance but allows individuals to purchase different amounts of insurance and to acquire care through the market from private providers independently of the insurance system. Private insurance companies offer varied insurance policies for different persons, depending in part on their desire and ability to pay. In this case not only does choice enter into the decision regarding the type of provider that best suits the individual, it can also affect the quality of care. Those with more wealth can afford to purchase more, better, or at least more expensive care.

Finally, health care can be wholly left to the market. This extends the arena of choice, for those who have the means, to the greatest possible degree. It assures choice in both senses – of kind of care and of quality. It makes the quality of care substantially dependent on desire and ability to pay.

Medical care bears a complex relationship to choice. The nature of my want often leaves me with little sense that I can choose. My want, then, is really a need, something imposed on me independently of my will. The classical economists, when they speak of subsistence, treat most of what workers want as things they need. They think of consumption in relation to the demands of the organism – for heat, nutrition, protection from the elements.

We experience our wants differently. We determine them for ourselves rather than taking them to be imposed on us. We make wanting part of our self-determination or self-expression. What we consume to satisfy wants cannot be determined independently of our will.

This does not mean that we are less interested in what we want than in what we need. Nor does it mean that what we want is not, in its own way, a requirement of our life. But, if it is a requirement of life, its demands are different from those imposed on us by the things we need.[5] The connection of choice to want marks this difference. Wants lead us to things we choose

---

[5] I discuss this in greater detail in Levine (1988, especially Chapter 1).

for ourselves as a way of expressing who we are. If it is important that we live a life expressive of who we are, then our wants are also important. To risk confusing matters a bit, we really do need the things we want, but in a different way.

The distinction between needs and wants is useful for thinking about the role of the market. Markets provide us with opportunities to acquire those consumption goods that suit us, express who we are, and enable us to live our lives. This aspect of the market underlies its connection with choice.

Those who advocate privatizing medical care emphasize choice. Opponents of privatization emphasize need. While often aware of the importance of choice (e.g., of doctor), they focus attention on the importance of providing medical care according to need rather than ability to pay. All citizens should receive care adequate to assist with whatever medical problem they have.[6]

If medical care is a need, then uniformity of provision (across persons, depending only on what is wrong with them and not on what they want) meets that need. If it is a want, uniformity does not. The issue rests on the role of self-determination and self-expression. The less central that role, the weaker the argument for privatization and associated market solutions.

If incomes vary, and we insist that medical care be acquired through the market, then the amount and quality of care must vary with income. Thus our classification of needs and wants bears on social policy, which will apply differently, depending on whether it concerns, or is thought to concern, needs or wants. The more we think in the language of want, the more we are likely to be satisfied by the idea that the free market should govern whether and how well we will be satisfied.

When we restrict attention to wants, problems still arise. If our needs were taken care of by nonmarket means, our wages would only affect satisfaction of wants. Our ability to satisfy wants will depend on the price of our capacities. Even if our needs are satisfied, our wants may not be. If wages are very unequal, and if some have other sources of income (from capital), then some have more choices than others. When ways of life vary dramatically with income, this can (as Veblen argues) affect what we want. Invidious comparisons between persons linked to levels of income and styles of life assure that many with lower incomes will end up wanting things others can afford but they cannot. Envy and resentment born of the dependence of livelihood on exchange can corrode the fabric of society.

In the case of need, the problem is how will society assure satisfaction where the argument for market provision looks weak. But when we think about wants, the market plays an important role. The question is not should

---

6 Obviously within limits sometimes hard to determine, as in the case of extraordinary measures for preservation of life.

we acquire the things to satisfy our wants outside the market. The element of choice at the center of want argues strongly against doing so. Rather, the question is what sorts of differences in want satisfaction are consistent with the kind of society we hope to live in. What differences do we value because we value our right to live different lives and be different people? And what sorts of differences do we judge harmful? How we answer these questions bears on what we judge to be the appropriate relation between private decisions and public responsibilities.

II

Capitalism

3

Capitalism

Making wealth

Adam Smith begins his exploration of the *Nature and Causes of the Wealth of Nations* by posing a question. What makes some nations poor and others wealthy, some savage and some civilized?[1] Smith tends to equate wealthy with civilized and refers to wealthy society as civilized society. Civilization is an important concept in political economy, although it seldom appears in modern writings. Civilized society provides its members with opportunities not otherwise available; but it also confronts them with dangers. This mix of risk and opportunity characterizes the economic system Smith links to the state of being "civilized."

For Smith, making wealth means producing wealth, and production means labor. The classical economists emphasized, more than we do today, labor's contribution to the production of wealth. Today, although labor remains important, we are also likely to emphasize the amount of capital stock (plant and equipment) and technical know-how. I will begin, however, with Smith's way of viewing the problem, which remains relevant.

Smith notices that some laboring produces wealth and some does not. We can work very hard and have little or much to show for it. If we think of work as expenditure of energy, we can expend the same amount of energy and produce no wealth, some wealth, or a great deal of wealth.[2] What decides the matter? Two attributes of our labor determine how much wealth, if any, we produce. One is whether we are trying to produce wealth. We can work

---

[1] For the moment, I take it for granted that we can usefully discuss problems of political economy in the context of the nation or state. The idea that the nation-state is the appropriate unit for addressing these problems has come under increasing criticism in recent years. Much of this criticism refers us to a perceived expansion in the interdependence of nations linked to economic ties, security considerations, environmental problems, and so on. In the first parts of this book I will not consider this set of issues, but continue to analyze the problems of political economy in a more classical vein.

[2] Work and labor are not necessarily the same (see Levine 1977, pp. 54–56).

with other purposes than producing wealth, purposes such as getting elected to office, cleaning our basement, having a good time. If we work toward these ends, we do not produce wealth. That we do not produce wealth does not make our activity unimportant. On the contrary, activities that do not produce wealth can be as or more significant than those that do: working for a nonprofit organization, learning to paint, engaging in political action. Producing wealth is a special sort of activity. It is one that employs some of our assets to produce commodities: goods and services valued in the market.

The other attribute of our labor relevant to how much wealth we produce is its productivity: In modern language, how efficiently do we work assuming that we are trying to produce wealth? Smith investigates both of these attributes of labor, beginning with the second.

According to Smith, labor's productivity depends on how it is organized and (less emphasized) what sorts of implements it has to work with. Smith refers to the manner of organizing labor as the *division of labor*. He regards the production process as a sequence of activities performed by workers using the tools and machinery available to them. Undivided labor refers to that way of organizing the sequence of tasks in which all are done by a single worker. Division of labor refers to that way of organizing labor that allocates different tasks to different workers. Smith's classic example is the division of labor in the production of pins:

One man draws out the wire, another straights it, a third cuts it, a fourth points it, a fifth grinds it at the top for receiving the head; to make the head requires two or three distinct operations; to put it on, is a peculiar business, to whiten the pins is another; it is even a trade by itself to put them into the paper; and the important business of making a pin is, in this manner, divided into about eighteen distinct operations, which, in some manufactories, are all performed by distinct hands, though in others the same man will sometimes perform two or three of them. (1776/1937, pp. 4–5)

According to Smith, the more we divide labor among specialized tasks, the more productive it will be. After the division of labor, each worker might make 4,800 pins in a day when he or she otherwise could not have made 20. The productivity of labor refers to the amount of output of some particular good producible by a unit of labor (say, an hour). How many pencils, loaves of bread, shirts, cars, can be produced by an hour's work? The more of each of these things (or others) we can produce in a given amount of time, the more productive our labor. Thus, if in an hour we can produce two loaves of bread, we are half as productive as we would be if we could produce four.[3]

Smith says that the more we specialize, the more efficient we become in

[3] If Y_i represents the output of good i, and L_i the labor time required to produce it, then the productivity of labor, say y_i is the ratio of the two:

$$y_i = Y_i/L_i$$

our tasks, the more productive we will be. Specialization is promoted by dividing up the labor into narrower tasks. The laborer would also become more productive if he or she were given better machines to work with. Smith mentions this but does not go into the matter at any length. A wealthy society is one in which labor works more rather than less efficiently, in which it is more rather than less productive – thus where the division of labor has advanced further.

But that is not the whole story. How wealthy a society can be also depends on whether its laborers are devoted to producing wealth or to some other end. Thus, for example, the more of the labor force we devote to the military, the less will be left over to produce wealth. Smith distinguishes between *productive* and *unproductive* labor according to whether the labor is devoted to producing goods and services whose sale will yield a profit.[4] Smith was especially concerned with the servant class, the clergy, and those working for government. He did not consider members of these classes productive laborers. The more of the work force engaged as servants to private households, the less was available for genuinely productive activities.

Thus, for Adam Smith, the nation's wealth depends on the proportion of its labor that is productive rather than unproductive and on the efficiency of the labor that is productive. The genius of the *Wealth of Nations* lies in its discovery of a single principle that, when applied to the organization of society, will encourage both greater efficiency of productive labor and the growth of the productive sector at the expense of the unproductive. This single principle is the following: Organize society around the purpose of profit seeking and wealth accumulation by placing society's productive resources into the hands of a group of persons (capitalists) devoted to seeking profit and accumulating wealth. When we do this, we orient our lives around pursuit of wealth. If successful, we become wealthy, individually and as a nation. But there is no guarantee of success.

Whether we succeed or fail, we must live with the people we make ourselves into by orienting our lives toward wealth as our goal. This is part of what we get when we become wealthy. A person concerned about the amount of his wealth, and how that amount measures up against the wealth of others, is a particular sort of person. A society that encourages members to adopt such concerns is a special sort of society. In a wealthy society, we are not simply people who have more wealth, we are people shaped to one degree or another by the nature of our interest in wealth.

---

[4] The problem of productive and unproductive labor in the classical theory is actually more complex than this. Smith uses the terms to mean different things at different points in his work. Sometimes he has in mind labor that produces goods, sometimes labor that produces value, and sometimes labor hired with an expectation that it will produce a profit for its employer.

Capital and labor

The classical economists answer the question of what makes a wealthy society by referring us to the design of an economic system. In other words
their answer centers on the way we organize our economic lives. Various
terms have been used to refer to the way of organizing our economic lives
that brings wealth and the capacity to produce wealth: capitalism, private
enterprise, and market economy. Because we are dealing with an economic
system, no simple definition can convey its full character or capture all its
vital dimensions. Capitalism has many features (see Marx 1867/1967, and
Heilbroner 1985), the most important of which involve who owns society's
productive assets and for what purpose. Let me begin with a definition that
links ownership of assets to income, as this will be of special importance
throughout our discussion. Later I consider the purpose served by private
ownership.

> *Capitalism* is an economic system in which the individual's income and
> wealth depend primarily on the value in the market of the property he
> or she owns (including the property we call labor).

One of the questions we will explore is that of the relation between this way
of organizing the economy and its capacity to produce wealth.

Our definition of capitalism suggests that we focus attention on how
private ownership encourages or impedes the growth of wealth. In modern
societies two kinds of property are of special importance: labor and the
means of production (especially plant, equipment, and material inputs).
Indeed, we could also define capitalism as an economic system in which
both labor and the means of production are the private property of particular persons or groups of persons. This definition is in some ways implied by
the above. Income and wealth come to depend on property ownership when
income-generating assets (especially labor and capital) are privately owned.
I begin my exploration of the capitalist economic system by briefly sum-
marizing some of what is implied when society organizes its economic life
through the buying and selling of labor and means of production.

In a capitalist economy, the worker's laboring capacity is a commodity
owned by the worker and sold by him in exchange for a wage. Economists
refer to the set of contracts trading laboring capacity for wages (money) as
the *labor market*. Although we can find exchanges of this type far back in
history, the organization of our economic lives through a set of such exchanges is a modern innovation (see Polanyi 1957).

By contrast, in a slave economy the worker is the property of the slave
owner. Workers are not free to sell their laboring capacities because they do
not own them. The master, who owns the slave, can sell (or possibly rent)

the slave to another. The master must support the slave much as he supports his livestock. The slave may be poorly treated and ill-fed, but not because his welfare depends on how much money he can get in exchange for his labor.

If the worker owns land and necessary inputs, he can produce what he needs. His livelihood need not depend on sale of his laboring capacity for a wage. The fact that he owns land and can produce what he needs frees him from dependence on the labor market. If he does not own land or other productive means, he has no alternative but to try to get his needs satisfied by selling what he does own: his laboring capacity.[5] In a capitalist economy, most people must sell their laboring capacity to secure their livelihood.

Making livelihood depend on the sale of labor is implied in the more general rule of capitalist economy: that your welfare should depend on the value of what you own (your assets). Assume for a moment that your most valuable asset is your laboring capacity. This happens to be true for most persons in capitalist economies. Then your livelihood depends on (1) whether you can find anyone interested in purchasing that asset from you, and (2) the price the asset brings when sold.

If you cannot sell your asset, then you are unemployed. If you can sell it but only at a low price, then you are poor even though employed. The organization of the labor market has much to do with the problems of poverty and unemployment. (We investigate that connection at greater length later on.) Throughout our investigation it is important to keep in mind that the problems of poverty and unemployment as we know them are linked to the way we organize our economies; they have to do with the dependence of livelihood on exchange and the fact that laboring capacity is the laborer's private property, often his most valuable asset.

The second market that distinguishes a capitalist economy is the market for *capital*. The term capital is somewhat complicated, especially in the way economists use it. In the following I emphasize two dimensions:

1. *Capital* is the wealth we use to acquire more wealth. In the language of the classical economists, it is wealth advanced or invested in the expectation of a return (an addition to wealth). Profit, dividends, capital gains, and interest are the return on the wealth – capital – invested in this way. We make profit when we sell goods at a price that exceeds the costs we incurred in producing them. We receive dividends as our part of the profit of a corporation in which we hold shares. We make capital gains when we sell capital (e.g., real estate or shares) at a price higher than that at which we bought it. We make interest when we lend money.

---

[5] For further discussion, see Polanyi (1944).

2. *Capital stock* is the means of production – plant and equipment – that produce goods and services. A printing press used to produce magazines for sale at a profit is capital stock.

In a capitalist society, most means of production are privately owned. Their owners keep them as part of their assets because they expect them to yield a profit.

In a modern capitalist economy, private ownership of the means of production takes a special form. The capital stock is owned by private corporations (or firms) rather than by persons. Shares in corporations are owned by individuals (or possibly by corporations or institutions). These shares are bought and sold in the stock market. The hope is that sale of the products of the capital stock will yield a profit to its owner, the corporation. The corporation then distributes a part of that profit – dividends – to its shareholders. The shareholders' dividends represent the return on their investment in the corporation.

The corporation solves an important problem. In a capitalist economy capital stock must be privately owned. But, for most persons, ownership of plant and equipment is not an attractive way to hold wealth. Many of us want or need to hold wealth in order to consume in the future income received today. For example, we intend to spend a part of today's income when we retire many years from now. Holding wealth means transferring purchasing power across time.

To do so, we could hold money, but holding capital has a decided advantage: the prospect that our purchasing power might grow as we hold it making it larger when we decide the time has come to use it. If we could hold capital, we would likely choose to do so. But holding capital stock is rarely a sensible option. First, it requires us to devote our time and energy to the management of the stock, a task for which we may have neither the interest nor competence. Second, the amount of wealth we have to invest is often inadequate to purchase capital stock. Thus we have an interest in owning capital without owning capital stock.

This interest can be satisfied if we can own shares in corporations rather than their productive assets. We then would own capital without owning capital stock, which the corporation would own. This solves the problem that someone must own society's capital stock even though few people can or want to own it. One result of this solution is a vast expansion of the market in which people buy and sell ownership shares in corporations (the stock market).[6]

[6] The expansion of the stock market has complex implications for the functioning of capitalist economy, as emphasized by Keynes (1936, Chapter 12); see also Minsky (1975).

Individuals may also lend money to corporations in the expectation of receiving interest rather than dividends. If they do, they have no ownership share in the corporation but only a legal claim to a return of their money with interest at a later point in time. What the creditor owns is a bond, or debt of the corporation. The money invested (whether as a loan or to acquire a share) is, by our definition, capital. The money used by the corporation to purchase its capital stock is capital for the corporation because it is an investment made with the expectation of profit.

In a capitalist economy, then, individuals have two ways of making money. They can sell their labor for a wage (or salary), and they can invest their wealth (if they have any) in capital hoping to make profit. Capital is valued according to the income it is expected to generate. The greater the return, the more valuable the asset. The firm owns capital stock not to consume its product, but because it hopes to sell that product and make profit. Profit making is the goal of production in a capitalist economy. Indeed, we can define capitalism as an economic system organized around production for profit. This has an important implication:

> In a capitalist economy, things are produced only if it is profitable to do so; and the amount produced depends on expected profitability.

Few things are more important in a capitalist economy than those that make certain activities more or less profitable. Thus, for example, it may not be profitable to produce long-term health care for the elderly, low-income housing, mass transportation, parks, or solar energy. In a capitalist economy, if profit cannot be made, goods will not be produced.

Profit is the difference between costs and revenue. *Costs* consist of the money paid for the needed inputs: the wages of labor, the price of materials (e.g., raw materials such as wood for making furniture and the electricity for running the machines), and a part of the price of the plant and equipment.[7] *Revenue* consists of receipts from sale of products. Thus

$$\text{Profit} = \text{revenue} - \text{costs}$$
$$\text{Revenue} = \text{amount sold} \times \text{price,}$$

Thus

$$\text{Profit} = (\text{amount sold} \times \text{price}) - \text{costs}$$

Benefits and harms of profit-driven production

Under capitalism, what is produced follows demand, which follows income.

[7] The part of the price of the plant and equipment referred to here is the depreciation of the capital stock. This element of cost must also be retrieved through the sale of the product.

Demand is the number of units of a good or service that can be sold at a given price. *Demand* is usually thought to vary with price, so that at higher (lower) prices demand will be lower (higher).

Thus

$$\text{Profit} = (\text{demand} \times \text{price}) - \text{cost}$$

Viewed from one angle, the link between demand and profitability assures that production responds to wants. So long as profitability is sensitive to demand and production is profit driven, producers will be motivated to produce those things consumers want, or at least those things consumers think they want and are willing to buy. This makes profit-driven production efficient in another sense emphasized by economists.

Efficiency refers to minimizing costs by making inputs, especially labor, as productive as possible. Efficiency means employing the least-cost methods available and, more importantly, reducing costs so far as possible. But, for many economists, efficiency also means adapting what is produced to the wants of those who will consume it. It would be inefficient to expend resources on turntables when consumers want compact disc players. Society needs to determine what commodities to produce and in what proportions. The economist's argument, going back to the period of Adam Smith, is that the market based on profit-oriented enterprise does just this. It automatically directs labor and other resources into those lines best suited to satisfy consumer wants.

Economists make much of the idea that a capitalist economy adapts production to wants. Exchange contracts are voluntary in a special sense. Legally, what we do with our incomes is up to us, so that when we purchase a commodity from its owner it is our decision to do so. In a market economy the element of consumer choice plays a large role. Because of this, it can be argued that what we consume in a market-oriented society is better adapted to what we want (or think we want) than it would be in the absence of a market. If we had no choice but to consume what the state provided, we would likely be less satisfied than we might be where we can take initiative in determining what we consume and therefore, to a degree, how we live.

The capitalist form of economic organization clearly has benefits, especially for those concerned with how we might become wealthy and thereby better satisfy our wants. But it also brings harms. The orientation of production toward ever greater profitability through lowering costs can imply little concern for human consequences.

It may be profitable to produce in a way that endangers the environment as exemplified by the destruction of the rain forests. Protecting the environment, on the other hand, may prove costly. One economist estimates the cost of a 50 percent reduction in the anthropogenic greenhouse gases responsible for global warming at $200 billion per year, or approximately 1 percent of world output (Nordhaus 1991).[8] If producers responsible for release of greenhouse gases are made to bear a share of this cost, this can adversely affect their profits. There are also costs involved in shifting refrigeration materials away from those that threaten the ozone layer, costs borne in part by producers (such as grocers) heavily dependent on refrigeration (Thayer 1990). To the capitalist, environmental protection can threaten profit. Business interests often oppose environmental regulations, which they see as a threat.

There may be other harms in profit-driven production. It may be more profitable to produce overseas leaving workers at home unemployed. When wages are significantly higher at home, cost-conscious producers can enhance their profit by producing abroad. This leaves the higher wage work force without employment. Because their livelihood depends on exchange, profit-driven production endangers their livelihood. These are some of the human consequences of profit-directed production. Political economy, in recent times, has paid special attention to some of these consequences.

The sensitivity of production to demand also brings harms. As we have seen, it provides a mechanism for adapting production to the wants of consumers as expressed in their willingness to part with their money in exchange for the goods produced. But it does so in proportion to the amount of money consumers have available. Those whose assets are inadequate will be unable to acquire an income capable of supporting a reasonable level of living.

It must be emphasized that demand in a capitalist economy is wants tied to dollars, and thus depends on income. This makes the system sensitive to inequalities of income. Those with little income have wants, but their wants do not translate into demand or influence production. They need adequate housing, but because they cannot pay for it, their need has no economic impact. Their need does not cause any housing to be produced.

The sensitivity of production to inequality follows from the treatment of human capacities as commodities valued in markets. Doing so is one of the most important characteristics of capitalism, and one of its most controversial.

The problem of benefits and costs of profit-oriented production is vitally important. Different orientations toward this problem help to define different attitudes toward capitalism. The classical liberals of the nineteenth century, including most economists of that period, tended to focus attention on the benefits as part of their special concern with how nations can become wealthy. They argued for introduction of the market institutions (private

---

[8] This author notes, however, that lower levels of reduction are much less costly, a 10 percent reduction costing less than $10 per ton ($CO_2$ equivalent).

property in land and means of production, minimum restrictions on trade, and so on) that they thought most likely to expand the wealth of nations. They favored, as do their modern counterparts, minimal government intervention.

Modern-day liberals favor an active government operating within the framework of capitalist economic organization. They emphasize the need to encourage profit seeking and the pursuit of greater efficiency in production through capitalistic economic organization while ameliorating some of its harms.

Socialists and other radicals emphasize the failure of a capitalist economy to deal with the human consequences of making production depend on profit and livelihood on exchange. They doubt the ability of capitalism to assure adequate living standards, and question the acceptability of the costs of making wealth accumulation the primary goal of economic life.[9]

I have described capitalism as an economic system organized to solve the problem posed by Adam Smith. This suggests that capitalism is a kind of historical invention. It did not always exist but had to be created. This does not mean that Adam Smith or any other individual invented capitalism. Smith was more an expositor and advocate than an inventor. Capitalism resulted from the actions of many individuals and groups over a long period of time. Relatively few of those responsible were aware that they were participating in a process of historical innovation. They mainly went about their business, looking after their own interests.

The struggle in which *The Wealth of Nations* played its part opposed two dramatically different ways of life, one on the decline, one on the rise (see Appleby 1984, and Polanyi 1957). The first emphasized social obligations to the members of the community, obligations of mutual dependence and work for collective goals. It emphasized personal connections, especially those linking family members. Self-seeking was, if not altogether repressed, restricted to a narrow part of life . The ends of the individual were tangled up with those of the community. The pursuit of self-interest was not considered an acceptable basis for building the edifice of an economic system for satisfying wants. It seemed hardly likely that self-interest would provide a strong basis for want satisfaction individually or collectively. It seemed much more likely to do harm.

The second way of life centered on self-interest and the market nexus. Relations between persons would be voluntary contracts between separate and independent proprietors. Emphasis would be placed on self-reliance and individual responsibility. The ends of community would disappear into

---

[9] Some also question the capacity of capitalism to assure the growth of the wealth of nations, especially for underdeveloped countries. For a classical statement, see Baran (1967).

wants that individuals defined for themselves. Want satisfaction would be contingent on market transactions.

The debate between these two ideals continues, if in a modified form. It underlies disputes over important issues in political economy. Those issues center on (1) how we view the obligations of individuals to the community and of the community to individuals, and (2) how we judge the idea that want satisfaction can and should be left up to the market, and thus made the outcome of private transactions entered into with no end other than self-interest.

4

The self-regulating market

Markets

The solution to the problem of how to create a wealthy society suggested in Chapter 3 is an institutional solution. That is, it proposes a way of organizing economic activity that will, more or less automatically, increase society's wealth. This organization makes the use of society's productive capacities (especially its capital stock and its labor) depend on private transactions (exchanges) between their owners.

Market refers to a set of exchange transactions by which money and goods change hands. This may be a subset of the exchanges entered into during a given period of time – for example, the labor market, the market for cars, the stock market. Or it may include all transactions undertaken during that period, in which case we refer simply to the market. A capitalist economy is a market economy par excellence. It organizes the bulk of economic activities through markets.

An important question to pose when we consider organizing our economic affairs through markets is whether doing so will work. That is, will private contracts undertaken to advance private interests assure that wants are satisfied? To satisfy wants, a complex set of goods must be produced and find their way from their producers to those who need them. Producers must be able to acquire needed inputs from those who own them. These inputs must be produced in quantities appropriate to assure adequate supply, and they must be available at prices that enable those needing the inputs to buy them given their incomes or revenues. These are not simple conditions.

If I produce bread for sale in my bakery, I must first purchase the flour, salt, sugar, butter, and so on, that I will need as inputs. Each of these goods must be available for purchase at a price I can afford, given the price at which I sell my bread. If I am a worker selling my laboring capacity, I must find a buyer (employer) who can afford to purchase my laboring capacity at a price (wage) that allows me to acquire the things I need. My wage must be at a level such that, given the prices of the things I need, I will be able to afford them.

Of course, bakers can judge their need for inputs according to more or less technical requirements linking amounts of flour, butter, salt, and so on, required to produce a loaf of bread and the number of loaves produced. In the worker's case things are somewhat more complicated. Defining how much a worker needs raises issues concerning the appropriate standard of living he or she might expect. A reasonable approach to this problem, and one favored by the classical economists, is to think about an expectable standard of living based on habits and experience built up in the past. Workers, then, are paid too little if they cannot maintain that expectable living standard, given wages and prices.

The problem briefly summarized here arises because want satisfaction depends on myriad private decisions. Wants form a system of mutual dependence of persons (including workers, consumers, producers) who must, in effect, work together even though no one coordinates what they do and no one is responsible for assuring that their decisions fit together. A capitalist economy is a system of private decisions having collective consequences. Political economy explores how those private decisions might or might not add up in such a way as to assure that wants are satisfied and that the wealth of the nation grows.

This exploration moves along two connected paths. The first has to do with the quantities of goods and labor made available and the relation of those quantities to the amounts needed. This is the relation of supply to demand. Private decisions do not add up in such a way as to assure want satisfaction if they lead to inadequate demand and thus unemployment. The second path has to do with the relation between the prices of goods and the wages of labor. Does this relation allow producers to cover their (wage) costs and make profit? Does it allow workers at least to maintain their expected standard of living? In the following, I consider these two questions.

The circular flow of economic life

Let us assume, for the moment, that consumers have more or less well-defined wants and that producers have adjusted their capital stock so that it is technically suitable to producing the kinds of things consumers want and in the proportions they want them. Thus, for example, producers know how many shoes (and of what types and sizes) will be needed (given the population) to replace the shoes that are wearing out. Producers have learned over time what to produce, say, by trial and error. So long as wants do not change much, production can be adjusted to them; and once adjusted, production need only be renewed from year to year. Doing so will, on average, enable people to get what they need to satisfy their wants. Economists would refer to this condition as a state of adjustment between demand and supply.

Supply refers to the output of goods available for sale in the market. We can refer to the supply of a particular good (bread, credit, labor), or we can refer to the supply of goods taken as a whole.[1]

In the state of adjustment producers know that the quantity produced is appropriate because each year demand for their goods is just adequate to absorb the supply. Because of this, each year they sell their goods (output) at prices adequate to enable them to cover their costs. When price at least covers costs, producers will receive revenue from sales adequate to renew their means of production and produce once again.

In important respects, market economies do, in fact, function this way. Firms have an idea based on past experience of what demand will be. The past is generally a useful guide to the future (one of the best under most circumstances). Everything works well so long as wants and methods of production do not change very much. But in market economies things sometimes change quite a bit.

Economic activity helps renew ways of life. By producing the appropriate goods and services and then distributing to those who need them, we re-create our ways of life from year to year. It is important to replace our cars when they wear out, to acquire a loaf of bread when we have eaten the one we had, to purchase a new pair of socks when the one we have is no longer useful. It is important for firms to hire the labor and purchase the materials required to produce our new socks, cars, loaves of bread. This renewal is not, however, simply a matter of habit; indeed, in a capitalist economy, habit never assures that appropriate decisions are made. That renewal is not simply a matter of habit is an important distinguishing characteristic of capitalism.

In a capitalist economy, renewal depends on a great many private decisions taken without any overall direction, plan, or control. Because of this, capitalism provides no overall assurance that wants will be satisfied. If wants are, by and large, satisfied, it is the result of decisions taken by independent property owners based on their self-interest rather than any interest in economic renewal, per se. In other words, the renewal of the economy as a whole must be the more or less automatic (and unintended) result of individuals acting without regard to it. This lack of conscious control, when it works, means that the market is self-regulating.

---

[1] In the following, I will use the term supply in a sense closer to that of the classical economists than to the modern usage. In particular, I will not assume that supply of goods is a function of price. Instead, I will generally treat it as adaptable, within limits, to fluctuations in demand. I explore this relation in greater detail later on.

The term *self-regulating market* refers to the market that brings about the satisfaction of wants through private production decisions taken on the basis of producers' private interests. The self-regulating market channels production in more or less appropriate directions and enables consumers to acquire the incomes they need to buy what they want.

The key components of the adjustment process are the following:[2]

1. Demand must be adequate to enable producers to sell goods at prices that cover costs and provide profit.
2. Incomes must be adequate given prices to allow consumers to buy what they need and thus secure their livelihoods. This means that (a) the demand for labor must be adequate to provide remunerative employment for workers or employees,[3] so they can acquire incomes and thus become consumers, and (b) the wage, the price of the worker's primary asset, must be adequate for acquisition of the goods that make up the worker's livelihood.
3. The ability to produce and thus supply goods must be roughly appropriate to the level of incomes and thus demand.

Market self-regulation poses a set of problems of coordination of decisions that jointly determine supply, demand, and prices for goods and labor.

The key to solving the problem of market self-regulation lies in the basic principle of a capitalist economy: Incomes derive from the sale of property. This fact of life under capitalism creates a circular relation between demand for products and demand for labor.

Hiring workers creates income, which creates demand for goods produced. When workers buy goods, they create revenues for producers that can be used to hire workers to renew, and possibly expand, the production of those goods. Thus, when workers buy goods they indirectly create demand for their own labor; and when firms hire workers they indirectly create demand for their own goods. I say indirectly because the causal circle only operates for the system of workers and firms taken as a whole. When the firm hires workers, it does not create demand for its products so much as it creates demand for other producers who, it hopes, in hiring workers will create demand for its products.

---

[2] It may seem unusual to those familiar with the standard account of market self-regulation that I do not include the matching between demand and supply in this list. The reason will become clear as we proceed. I do not assume that it is part of the function of a capitalist market to match supply and demand, especially in the short run. This does not mean that the relation between the two is unimportant.

[3] I use the terms worker and employee more or less interchangeably.

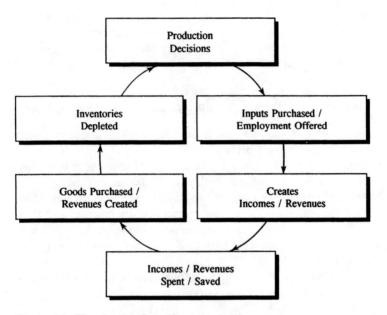

Figure 4.1. The circular flow of economic life.

The demand thus created signals the need to produce more. One such signal involves running down inventories of produced goods. Depletion of inventories indicates the need to produce more.

We will consider some implications further on. But for the moment, let me summarize the circular flow in a simple diagram. Figure 4.1 represents the *circular flow of economic life*. It includes a process of circular causation vital to the self-regulating capacity of market economies.

Movements within the circular flow are movements of goods and money through a sequence of exchanges. We can view the circuit as a flow of money. By following the money flow, we can trace out the way in which each moment leads to the next. We began with hiring decisions of producers. But, because we also ended with hiring decisions, it should be clear that it makes no difference where we begin. The flow has no real beginning and no real end point.

When firms hire workers, they place money into the hands of those who make their laboring capacity available for production. Thus two results follow from this step in the circular flow: the creation of incomes and the production of commodities. Production of commodities creates supply; receipt of incomes creates demand. Workers, in their capacity as consumers, use their incomes to purchase the goods they themselves produce. This creates a demand to absorb the supply of goods whose production was the original motive driving producers to hire the workers.

Purchase of goods from firms creates revenues and profits for them. The money that came into the hands of workers when they sold their laboring capacity to producers now flows back to the producers in exchange for consumption goods bought by workers. This return flow makes it possible for producers to hire workers once again, setting the process in motion through another circuit. Purchase of goods simultaneously accomplishes two tasks required to keep the flow moving. It places money needed to hire workers into the hands of producers, and it absorbs the current supply of goods justifying producers in rehiring workers. Without demand for current output, producers would have no reason to produce more output for future demand. Hiring decisions and therefore employment depend on demand.

In 1933, at the height of the Great Depression, the U.S. steel industry produced 23.2 million (gross) tons of steel, when, given the capital stock available and its productivity, that industry could have produced 70.2 million tons (Steindl 1952, p. 6). Output of steel was a third of what it could have been. At the same time, the aggregate unemployment rate was 24.9 percent (U.S. Department of Commerce 1975). Demand for steel suffered due to the failure of demand for goods that employed steel as an input. In the early 1930s the average age of cars owned increased as the ability of consumers to purchase new cars deteriorated (Bernstein 1987, pp. 58–59). Because approximately 18 percent of steel output was, at the time, used in production of cars (Bernstein 1987, p. 55), a failure in consumers' capacity to purchase cars could not but have a significant impact on the level of production in the steel industry. But the fall in steel production meant high levels of unemployment in that industry. Low levels of production are both cause and effect of low levels of employment.

The circular flow depicted in Figure 4.1 is the circular flow of the economy as a whole. The demand created by the hiring and production decisions of the individual firm creates incomes used to buy goods produced by other firms. Thus, each producer and consumer depends on the system of producers and consumers considered as a whole. Decisions of others (whom we do not even know) determine our ability to gain employment, receive income, and produce goods.

Price determination

Adequate productive capacity and demand make it possible for workers and producers to acquire the things they need. But adequate demand is also a matter of the relation of price to income, or of the prices of goods to the price of labor. Goods supplied must be available at appropriate prices. How might this condition be satisfied?

The answer depends on the kind of product and the nature of the market in which it is sold. Price determination differs, depending on whether or not the product is reproducible and the supply expandable to meet changes in demand.[4]

Consider manufactured goods. Producers of manufactured goods must have or acquire three kinds of inputs: labor, raw materials, and capital stock. In general, it is costly and time-consuming to change the amount of capital stock. But it is possible to use the same capital stock to produce different amounts of output by operating it more or less intensively. Thus an auto assembly line might run a few hours a day, all day and well into the night, or not at all, depending on how much output the firm expects to sell.

> We refer to the intensity of use of the capital stock as its rate of *capacity utilization*. If we think of the maximum sustainable level of utilization as full capacity, we can measure capacity utilization as the ratio of output actually produced to the amount that could be produced at full utilization.

Figure 4.2 presents data on capacity utilization in U.S. manufactures. It should be clear from the data that utilization varies over time and that the capital stock is normally operated at less than full capacity. Indeed, the data indicate a slight downward trend in percent of capacity used since the end of World War II.

As utilization varies, the amount of capital stock remains fixed, but the amounts of labor and materials used vary. Economists refer to inputs whose employment varies with the level of production as *variable* or *prime* costs. The inputs that cannot be changed to meet changes in current market conditions are *fixed* or *overhead* costs.

Manufactured goods can be produced in varying quantities, so producers may purchase (variable) inputs as needed to meet demand. Supply of agricultural products is not so easily adjusted. Once farmers decide to plant so much wheat, for example, the amount they get cannot be altered much by subsequent decisions. If you produce the kind of tomatoes sold fresh in the supermarket rather than the kind put into cans and made into sauce, you must sell your tomatoes when they are ripe. Earlier or later, they will have no value. This means that you cannot adjust supply to current demand conditions by changing how much labor you employ and how intensively you use your capital stock (or, in this case, land). If you produce cars, you have more

---

[4] This distinction is emphasized by Michal Kalecki (1965).

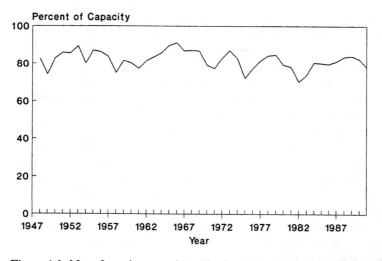

Figure 4.2. Manufacturing capacity utilization rates, 1948–1989. *Source:* Economic Report of the President, 1990, 1992.

flexibility regarding when they are sold. Holding for lengthy periods of time may be costly, but the car does not rapidly lose all its value.

The ability of manufacturers to adjust production to demand has an important implication.[5] They can, within limits, set prices they deem acceptable and refrain from selling their products until someone comes along prepared to pay the price. In manufacturing, the problem of assuring that price covers cost can generally be solved by having the producer set the price. Then the problem is assuring demand given that price. In manufacturing, supply rather than price varies with demand. As a result, the level of production varies with demand, and so does the level of employment.

In manufacturing the producer sets the price in relation to his costs of production. The price allows the seller to cover his costs and turn a profit. The margin between price and cost is the profit margin. The seller can then be said to set the price by "marking up" the costs by the amount of the profit margin. The price depends on the per unit costs and on the size of the markup or margin for profit.

---

[5] The ability of the producer to set price clearly also depends on his relationship with the seller. If the producer is the seller, and if he is not constrained to sell off his inventory at once, then he can set the price and allow sales rather than price to fluctuate. If, however, the producer supplies a retailer who takes his supplies from many competing producers, the retailer (or other middleman) has leverage to force the producer to cut price when demand flags. See Kaldor (1985).

This way of thinking about market adjustment differs from that common in textbooks, and it may be worthwhile to briefly review the difference. The textbook interpretation of market adjustment assumes that supply (e.g., limited available inputs – resources or factors of production) constrains output and consumption. Supply constraints imply that higher levels of demand mean higher costs of production. If demand for a product increases, supply cannot adjust except by using less efficient inputs and incurring higher costs. Thus either potential consumers must be turned away (made to queue up for the available output), or the price must rise to cover increasing production cost. The higher price excludes those consumers whose income does not allow them to afford the good (in the economist's language, the price runs up against the consumer's "budget constraint"), or it simply encourages some consumers to substitute other less costly items. Similarly, when demand for a good is low, a lower price will make it affordable to more consumers or encourage them to substitute in its favor. This will increase demand until it meets the supply (or resource) constraint.

In this sort of world, price plays the pivotal role in assuring that available resources are fully utilized and in signaling producers what and how much of different goods to produce. The key problem is not how much to produce overall (and thus how much employment to offer) but how to distribute resources among alternative uses. The prevailing idea is that the allocation of resources in the production of different goods (shoes, cars, hospital beds, parks) should accord with the wants or desires of consumers (given their incomes).

The market works differently when we assume, as I will in this book, that the economy is not supply constrained but normally operates with excess capacity. Excess capacity allows producers to adjust output rather than price in response to changes in demand.[6] Prices remain important for accomplishing two ends (see Levine 1988, chapter 4). First, they assure that producers can make profit (more on this in the next chapter). Second, they assure access to goods by consumers given their incomes. Price, then, intermediates between the producer's need to cover costs and make profit and the consumer's need to acquire the good given its price and his or her income.

Why assume that production is demand constrained rather than limited by capacity? One answer is that a demand-constrained system has decided advantages for producers and consumers. These advantages stem from greater price stability in demand-constrained systems.

Price volatility can make planning difficult and undermine the security of producers and consumers. For consumers, price vitally affects livelihood.

---

[6] For discussion of the justification for this viewpoint, see Kaldor (1985, pp. 35–7) and Nell (1988).

For them, price should be linked to income levels rather than short-run fluctuations in demand. Consumers prefer suppliers who can maintain more or less stable prices. Producers concerned with customer loyalty strive to stabilize prices and assure adequate supply in the face of demand fluctuations (see Okun 1981).

5

Creative destruction

Innovation

Change under capitalism is not accidental. Change, from poor to wealthy society, is the purpose of capitalist economic organization. This means change in what and how much we produce and consume, change in our methods of production, and change in the way we organize the production process. If all market economy did was assure satisfaction of unchanging wants by unchanging means, it would not be the answer to Adam Smith's question: How do we create a wealthy society? The problem is not, then, satisfaction of habit-dominated wants but adjustment to change. The change that a capitalist market economy must adjust to is change brought about to enhance the profitability of capitalist enterprise. The profit motive lies at the heart of the process of growth and development of a capitalist economy.

In a capitalist economy, the agent that brings about change is the capitalist enterprise and especially the capitalist entrepreneur.[1]

> An *entrepreneur* is an individual or group that introduces a change in what is produced, how it is produced, or how it is sold.

Because the entrepreneur is driven by a desire for profit, the change brought about must hold the promise of yielding a profit otherwise unavailable.

The profit motive is central to the behavior of the entrepreneur; but it does not wholly explain why he does what he does. In a broader view, the entrepreneur is motivated to reorganize and redirect society's energies along new paths. Profit is as much means as end. Without profit, the entrepreneur cannot be the agent of change. And, of course, if the entrepreneur gets rich along the way, this is not by accident, nor is it irrelevant to why he does what he does.

[1] The classic discussion is that of Joseph Schumpeter (1934).

The entrepreneur might have a new way to produce an existing good at significantly lower cost than that incurred by its current producers. Lower cost might result from technical change (see Rosenberg 1971, 1976).

Technical change refers to a change in the way goods are produced. It may be a change in the machinery or other equipment employed, for example, from hand stitching to the use of a sewing machine or from a typewriter to a word processor. Such a change might increase the productivity of labor or improve the quality of the product. Technical change can also be organizational. Adam Smith's notion of the division of labor was at heart an organizational change in the method of production designed to enhance the productivity of labor. The introduction of the assembly line, and the more recent movement away from it, are examples of organizational changes (which also affect equipment, of course). When productivity rises, unit costs decline and, other things equal, profit increases.

Technical change is not the only avenue to increased profitability. Entrepreneurs may have ideas for new consumer goods. If consumers' incomes are rising, or if they can be induced to substitute new goods for old, product innovation offers opportunity for profit making and market expansion (see Levine 1988, Chapter 4).

The possibility of innovation in methods and products has two important implications for profit-seeking capitalists. First, their profit is not determined for them. It depends on their skill (and luck) in discovering and introducing lower-cost methods of production, cheaper sources of inputs, and new consumer goods. The dependence of profit on innovation links the profit motive to economic development and the growth of wealth. The second implication is that the profits currently made by capitalists producing for established markets in established ways are always insecure. There is an ever present danger that an entrepreneur will introduce better products or more productive techniques. Doing so can take away part of the demand for established products, reducing or eliminating their producer's profit.

Competition

We refer to the process by which sellers attempt to bring about a shift in demand favorable to them as *competition*. Competition is born of the pursuit of profit in unregulated markets. It intensifies the pressure on firms to be more productive and to produce goods better suited to the perceived wants of consumers.[2]

---

[2] For classic discussions, see Chamberlin (1933) and McNulty (1968). On the process of competition in capitalist economies, see Levine (1981, Chapters 4 and 5) and Steindl (1952).

In Chapter 4 I indicated that prices depend on costs and markups. Given, however, the producer's interest in profit, the greater his markup the better his interest is served, all else equal. What, then, limits the markup and thus the firm's profit and the price at which it sells its product? Price competition establishes such limits. It translates the seller's concern with demand into an upper limit on price. It does so because the firm assumes that demand and price are connected.

The connection between demand and price has two roots. First, the higher the price, the less affordable the product. At lower prices more consumers can afford to buy, and thus demand will be greater. Second, a higher price causes a problem when other producers of the same or comparable goods offer theirs at a lower price. Consumers choose the lower-priced goods, eroding the market of the higher-price seller. In brief, competition limits prices and profit margins.

The level of price depends on costs and competitive conditions. The more likely that a higher price will lead to loss of demand to competitors, the more inclined the seller to maintain a smaller margin over cost in order to protect his market. Because demand limits price, the price system is responsive to consumers' wants. Products tend to be priced at levels that make them accessible. This solves, at least in principle, an important part of the problem of self-regulation.

Price competition follows cost advantages gained by producers who introduce new, more productive techniques.[3] If producers sell the same or similar goods at the same price, those with the lower cost will make a greater profit. This greater profit can be used to increase the lower-cost producer's *market share*. The firm's market share is the ratio of its sales of a good to the total market for that good. A firm can use its cost advantage to enhance its market share by financing a costly advertising campaign beyond the means of the higher-cost (lower-profit) competitor. Alternatively, the lower-cost producer can offer his product at a lower price. Doing so means lower per unit profit, but the lower price may increase market share and thus the amount sold and the total profit (profit per unit multiplied by the number of units sold).

In many cases the level of demand for a product varies inversely with its price. That is, demand rises as price falls and falls as price rises. One reason for this is that as price falls, more consumers can afford the product, given their incomes. Another reason is that as the producer lowers his price, he may be able to attract customers away from his higher-priced competitors and thus increase his market share. If demand for the firm's product rises as

---

[3] Price competition is not the only, or in all cases the most important, kind of competition. Producers also compete to produce better, or at least more attractive, products. I emphasize price competition here to highlight the relation of competition to real incomes.

its price falls, producers may have an incentive to lower their prices (if the fall in per unit profit does not more than offset the impact of higher sales volume on total profit). If the cost of production falls due to technical innovation, then producers have the means to lower prices and thus increase their markets. The more efficient producer, then, can increase his market at the expense of his competitors. When this happens, prices fall and consumers' real incomes rise.

> *Money income* refers to income as defined earlier, a sum of money. *Real income* refers to the purchasing power of money income given prices. Thus real income will double if the prices of the goods the consumer buys are halved.

Competition leads to growing real incomes. The price system, then, serves two important social purposes. First, it enhances individual welfare by allowing consumers to choose what they will consume and thereby adapt their consumption to their wants. Second, it translates productivity gains into real income gains.

Profit seeking is the motor force of the price system. What is produced, how much is produced, and how it is produced all depend on a calculation of profitability. Producers will devote their resources to those lines of production likely to yield the greatest profit. They will employ the most profitable technique available to them. They will produce only as much as they think they can profitably sell.

The level of demand, the costs of production, and the price of the product together determine profitability. The profit motive drives investors to place capital where demand is robust and goods can be sold at prices that, given costs, yield profit. This suggests that the profit motive serves an organizing function in market economy. The profit motive organizes the process of development in a decentralized economy of uncoordinated private decisions.

Let me briefly summarize the link between competition and the solution to Adam Smith's problem, how to create a wealthy society. Capitalism organizes production around the pursuit of profit. The pursuit of profit leads producers to seek more productive methods and more attractive products. Introduction of new means of production – technical innovation – lowers costs and increases profit. The producer's concern with markets limits the margin of price over cost and acts as an incentive to keep prices down. It also encourages producers to lower prices when costs fall, especially in highly competitive environments.

Adjustment of prices to lower costs transforms higher profit due to productivity increase into higher living standards for consumers. In the economist's language, competition brings a distribution of the fruits of technical progress from seller to consumer.

On one side, competition is the process by which producers hope to make greater profit by increasing their market shares. On the other side, competition increases the level of demand for products by raising consumers' real incomes. By driving down the price, competition increases the purchasing power of the consumer's money income. Thus competition simultaneously exploits and creates the market.

This process has an additional benefit. Assume that consumers spend their incomes on the things they need to maintain their ways of life. If so, incomes are, in effect, committed to replacing the goods they have used up. But this restricts demand to existing channels and precludes innovation in modes of consumption. It severely limits capitalist growth and development.

For economic development to take place, consumers need to find part of their incomes uncommitted to replacing those things needed to renew ways of life.[4] Competition can create this uncommitted income by lowering the cost of goods consumed, thus creating a margin between our money income and the cost of renewing our way of life. This is another way of talking about the increase in real income that comes about when prices fall.

Economic development

Joseph Schumpeter refers to the processes described in this chapter as "creative destruction" (1950). By creating new technology, new consumer goods, and new forms of economic organization, capitalism destroys older methods of production and ways of life. Schumpeter understands capitalism as a system of economic change and development. This vision of capitalism originates with the classical economists, especially Adam Smith. But, during the classical period, it was Karl Marx who understood best the significance of capitalism to human progress. In Marx's words, under capitalism

[a]ll fixed, fast frozen relations, with their train of ancient and venerable prejudices and opinions, are swept away, all new-formed ones become antiquated before they can ossify. All that is solid melts into air, all that is holy is profaned. (1972/1848, p. 476)

Capitalism carries us at rapid pace from past to future. The way we live is constantly subject to challenge. Our livelihood is rarely secure. The mix of creation and destruction makes insecurity a cost of progress. The economic system – capitalism – that makes us wealthy does not make our wealth secure. Yet, this very insecurity, by allowing change, has its contribution to make.

In Chapter 2 I emphasize the connection between wealth and security. Capitalism promotes the growth of wealth and thus increases the potential

---

[4] I have developed this notion at greater length Levine elsewhere (see Levine 1981, Chapter 4).

security society provides its members. But, because of the way it goes about increasing social wealth, capitalism also fosters insecurity. This is no longer insecurity born, for example, of the vagaries of climate, but insecurity born of the organization of an economic system. That system fosters economic development often at the expense of ways of life dependent on structures made obsolete by economic development.

The new, more productive technique makes the old superfluous. In doing so, it makes the labor involved with the old technique superfluous as well. Change enriches some while impoverishing others. The human consequences of the struggle between the old and new – the process of creative destruction – challenge political economy. Can we alleviate the suffering caused by change without crippling the forces of change? What modifications in our economy will likely do so? If we cannot deal with the human consequences of creative destruction without harming that process, how shall we determine the trade-off between the benefits of creation and harms of destruction?

The vision summarized in this and the previous chapter carries a strong judgment concerning the virtues of capitalism. First, an economy organized through unregulated ("free") markets is capable of assuring the production of things people need and getting those things from producers to consumers. Second, such an economy accomplishes important goals by transforming a poor society into a wealthy one.

Smith speaks of this transformation as a social good or public end accomplished as an unintended consequence of the pursuit of private interest. Smith formulates this feature of a capitalist economy in striking language. Under capitalism, we pursue our private interests with no consideration for the interests of others or the good of society as a whole. The interests of others are only relevant to us when we need something they have to satisfy our wants. The baker depends on the consumer as market for his products; the butcher depends on the rancher for the meat he prepares for his customers. To get others to help satisfy our wants, we appeal to their self-interest. Their self-interest drives them to buy from us what we want to sell or sell to us what we want to buy. Yet, according to Smith, this pursuit of self-interest leads to the common good.

It does so for two interconnected reasons. First, as suggested in the previous paragraph, our self-interest drives us to serve others. We produce what market demand signals us to produce and market demand derives from the wants and needs of others. The market disciplines us to translate our self-interest into a concern with the interest of others, even though this interest is essentially instrumental. It is instrumental in that our concern with the wants of others stems not from a concern with their welfare per se but from our concern with our own welfare and a recognition that serving theirs will serve ours.

Second, pursuit of our interests drives us to seek profitable ventures in which to invest our wealth. Profit seeking impels us to organize enterprise in ever more productive and efficient forms. Society's capital stock is the means it has available to satisfy needs. Capitalism places society's capital into private hands, subjecting it to private decisions based on private interest. Will those who own the capital stock as their private property use it in ways most likely to maintain and enhance it? Smith's answer is yes. In a capitalist economy, the owners of capital are driven to employ it where it will be as productive as possible.

Smith argues that the state could do no better. The result of private ownership is investment of wealth where it is most likely to enhance society's producing potential. If this is the public good then, Smith claims, it can be accomplished by private means, without government intervention.

We may have cause to doubt this item in Smith's case for the self-regulating market. One question concerns a potential difference between the motives of private persons and those of the state. If the state concerns itself with the larger good of the group as a whole, or with securing ideals the nation values, this may lead in directions different from those taken by individual citizens.

Individual citizens may find it more to their benefit to use wilderness areas for commercial development offering the prospect of private gain to developers. If, however, we as a society value protection of the natural environment, our collective ends can conflict with those of private entrepreneurs.

Private persons are interested to invest their capital in the most profitable lines, but they have no reason to invest at home when those more profitable lines are elsewhere. Smith, somewhat quaintly, thought that investors would prefer to invest at home where they were more secure or as an expression of national feeling. Since publication of the *Wealth of Nations*, national feeling has proven a very limited force where investment is concerned. (I return to this problem in Part IV.)

Smith favored the private solution because he assumed people act out of self-interest. The problem for him was not to correct this defect in human nature (if it is a defect) but to make it work for the greater good. Smith had considerable contempt for government, in part because he saw in it a vehicle by which politicians pursue their private ends rather than the public good. Smith believed that there is indeed a public good; and this posed a dilemma, given his convictions about the role of self-interest in human motivation. He thought that we cannot count on individuals giving up private interest for the public good; all we can do is arrange our institutions so that pursuit of private interest leads to the public good.

6

Labor

Wages

As I have emphasized, a capitalist economy is one in which one's welfare depends on the value in the market of the assets that one owns. In this chapter I consider the challenge making welfare depend on exchange poses for those whose income depends on sale of their laboring capacity.

This is a particularly important problem for political economy. In a capitalist economy, the wage is the price of a commodity. If the price is set by the market, and without government regulation, what will assure that it is adequate to allow the worker to purchase the things he or she needs? Even if the price is appropriate, will the demand for labor be sufficient to assure that all those who depend on wages for their livelihood will find employment?

First, we need to consider what constitutes an adequate wage. For manufactured goods, we can more or less easily determine what price is adequate to the seller if we know the costs of production. The price must at least cover those costs, which depend primarily on the nature of the plant and equipment, the cost of material inputs, and the cost and quality of labor. Can we make any comparable calculation for labor?

The classical economists thought we could. Adam Smith, David Ricardo, and Karl Marx all argued that labor has a cost of production "like all other things which are purchased and sold" (Ricardo 1951, p. 93). This cost was assumed to be the goods required for workers to continue their lives and that of their families in ways consistent with an historically and culturally determined standard. As we have seen, the classical economists called this standard the "subsistence." In the first instance, the subsistence consists of a set (sometimes referred to as a basket) of goods: so much bread, so much clothing, so much heat for the home. The list varies across time and place, but given that list, it would be possible to calculate the level of the wage needed to assure that when livelihood depends on exchange, exchange will provide livelihood.

The money wage must equal the sum of the prices of the goods included in the subsistence basket. This idea of subsistence bears a relationship to the modern notion of the "poverty level" (discussed in Chapter 10). Setting a poverty level strikes many as arbitrary, and the notion of subsistence seems likewise difficult to pin down. The difficulty results from the fact that meaningful definitions of a subsistence minimum must call on what we know about existing, in a sense habitual, ways of life. The goods that make up the subsistence (clothing, food, shelter) do not exist as abstract amounts of nutrition and warmth but as concrete items normally used to satisfy wants.

Because of this, the only way we can know the subsistence level is by considering our own basic consumption habits. This carries forward the classical idea that subsistence is the habitual level of life. Thinking this way tells us something important about wages. Current living standards, if maintained long enough, become the expected standards and tell us how much the worker must be paid if the market is to succeed in providing an "adequate" livelihood. Stagnation of real incomes means the market has failed. We can now restate the challenge posed by the wage for capitalist economic organization. How does a capitalist economy assure that real incomes of those whose primary asset is their laboring capacity will at least be maintained at their habitual levels?

The process of creative destruction provides part of an answer to this question. The drive to increase productivity and improve product quality, combined with competition over markets, leads firms to make their products more affordable. On the firm's side, the resulting market growth leads to more profit and investment. On the consumer's side, competition that lowers prices raises living standards. So far as creative destruction brings with it a rising trend in living standards it assures that habitual levels of living do not erode and workers are provided their subsistence (and more).

This works because the wage is not only the worker's income and a cost of production, it is also a primary source of demand. In the circular flow the creation of incomes also creates demand for goods. The producer's concern to increase demand for his product leads him to do things (e.g., lowering his price) that increase the real wage.

The historical trend toward improved living standards has made the classical notion of subsistence sound archaic, at least for the more advanced capitalist economies. We have come to expect living standards to increase over time. As a result, we now treat success in assuring a habitual level of living as no success at all.

I think this judgment carries some force. Recall the earlier discussion of the importance of change in justifying capitalist economic organization. The connection between markets and economic development lends conviction

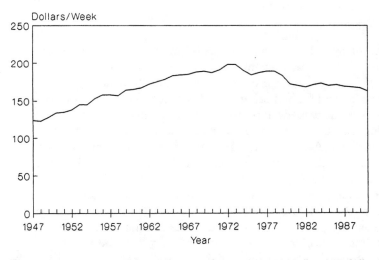

Figure 6.1. Average weekly earning, nonfarm, 1947–1990 (in 1977 dollars). *Source:* Economic Report of the President, 1990, 1992.

to claims about their virtues. When incomes stagnate, ways of life become fixed, and thus capitalist economic organization loses much of its appeal.

This suggests that we redefine the classical notion of subsistence, so far as it is applied to capitalist economy, to include not only assurance of current standards but also provision of a margin for improvement. The market has met the challenge posed by making livelihood depend on exchange when it improves living standards, and the market should be judged by its capacity to bring about such improvement.

Figure 6.1 gives a rough indication of the success and failure of the U.S. economy according to this standard. Over the long run, living standards improved dramatically, and it can be said that capitalism has met the challenge if not for all those dependent on it, certainly for a great many. At the same time, there have been periods of failure. More worrisome is the recent trend. Expectations of continuing improvement will surely be disappointed if failure over the past years continues into the future. If the trend toward improved living standards is over, what will this mean for our commitment to having livelihood depend on exchange?

These trends, of course, cover the majority of workers. But many fall by the wayside; and even those doing well can suffer hard times. The upward trend should not allow us to forget the periods of high unemployment or the large numbers of those left out. In subsequent chapters I consider these darker realities of capitalist economy.

Laboring capacity

Because the price of labor, unlike prices of other goods, is the worker's lifeline, many have argued against treating laboring capacity as a commodity. Karl Marx denounced capitalist economy for treating the worker like a commodity and for harboring the illusion that the worker's ownership of his laboring capacity made him a free person, a commodity owner just like the capitalist who buys the laboring capacity at its price, the wage. Karl Polanyi argued that labor was a "fictitious commodity." Although it is legally and practically treated as a commodity (it is bought and sold), doing so threatens the laborer's integrity.

However we judge the success of capitalism over the long run, we cannot entirely escape the problems posed by its treatment of labor as a commodity or avoid recognizing that responsibility for welfare cannot simply be left to the market. Examples of acknowledgment of the limits of the wage contract as the guarantor of income include minimum wage laws and provision of welfare for those who cannot get adequate pay for their labor. These are examples of government intervention aimed at preventing undue hardship for those dependent on the market for their livelihood.

The idea that laboring capacity can be treated as a commodity only at some peril provides justification for limiting the market and widening public responsibility. Not all, however, favor intervention to regulate the wage contract and assure a safety net for those unable to acquire their livelihood through exchange. Some see in measures limiting the market a threat to the vitality of the economy.

Measures that secure incomes might endanger competitiveness. When we must compete with producers whose labor costs are a fraction of our own, the more we recognize the demand to secure an expected living standard, the more we endanger our competitive position. In 1991, hourly compensation for Mexican workers was 12 percent of that of U.S. workers (see Figure 11.2). The less the labor market disciplines workers to provide their labor at a cost consistent with competition (including competition from overseas) and profit making, the less viable the economy in a competitive world market.

Recall that the wage serves three functions: It is the livelihood of the worker, a cost of production, and a source of demand. The first and third functions are best served when government protects incomes and when real wages rise over time. The second is not. There is then a built in tension in the wage system resulting from its multiple functions. The economy becomes an object of political debate and conflict as different groups focus on different functions and arrive at different judgments of the best configuration of the labor market to serve the function they consider most important.

Figure 6.2. U.S. unemployment rates, 1960–1991. *Source:* Economic Report of the President, 1990, 1992.

Unemployment

Figure 6.2 presents historical data on unemployment in the United States. Historically, the United States experiences levels of unemployment below 4 percent only during wartime expansion of the armed forces (World War II, the Korean War, and the Vietnam War).[1] Average United States unemployment rates were 4.8 percent in 1960–69, 6.2 percent in 1970–79, and 7.3 percent in 1980–89.

Employment follows the demand for labor. The demand for labor refers to the sum of employment provided individually by capitalist firms. Of course, substantial employment is also offered in the public and nonprofit sectors. Still, the private sector remains the primary engine of employment in capitalist economies.

Each firm makes its own decision regarding employment. This decision is constrained by two primary considerations: the plant and equipment the firm owns – its capital stock – and the firm's expectations concerning demand for its products.

---

[1] Statistics on unemployment can be misleading because they only treat those actually looking for work as part of the unemployed. Those who have become discouraged about finding employment are not counted as unemployed workers. Thus the unemployment rate normally reported in the press understates the magnitude of the problem.

When demand for the firm's products is sufficient to justify it operating at or near full capacity, the firm can only add to its demand for labor by adding to its capital stock. Demand for labor follows capital accumulation, growing more or less in step with the growth in capital (the rate of investment). The classical economists emphasized this side of the demand for labor and tended to attribute any excess supply of labor (state of demand inadequate to maintain full employment of labor) to an inadequate accumulation of capital.

As we have seen, firms do not always, or very often, operate at full capacity. Firms may operate at less than full capacity because of aggregate demand failure or for reasons peculiar to their industry and the state of competition. Some of the reasons for firms operating below full capacity include the need to maintain reserves of capacity to deal with seasonal and other anticipated fluctuations in demand, adverse economic conditions such as recession or competitive failures, and a desire to be prepared to meet growth in demand with capacity already in place (build capacity ahead of demand). When these considerations prevail, the level of employment offered by firms is not constrained by the amount of capital stock but by its level of utilization.

The most important factor affecting the firm's level of utilization is the demand for its products. Firms may be stuck with capital stock whether or not demand exists for their products. But they are not (in general) stuck with a fixed labor force. Firms do what they can to adjust their levels of employment to the demand for their products.[2] Inadequate demand can stem from a low level of economic activity or from erosion in market share due either to erosion in the industry's share of overall market demand or erosion in the firm's share of industry demand.

The labor market

Our brief survey of the causes of unemployment raises a question. From the standpoint of a market economy, we can think of the labor market as much like other markets in that it counterposes supply and demand for a commodity, labor. The supply of labor consists of those seeking work as a way of providing income needed for their livelihood. The demand for labor follows the needs of producers for the labor input. Unemployment means excess supply. More laborers are seeking work than are needed by producers.

In goods markets, firms experiencing excess supply cut back on levels of production. Obviously, laborers cannot do this because their livelihood de-

---

[2] An important part of the labor force works for a salary and not a wage. The difference affects the point made in this paragraph because the demand for salaried employees does not move in any simple way with demand for the firm's product.

pends on exchange. What market response does excess supply in the labor market stimulate, and can that response help correct the maladjustment between supply and demand?

If it could, this would be important. It would mean that the labor market will automatically (i.e., without government intervention) adjust supply of and demand for labor. If supply equals demand, then employment is available to all seeking it. The free market would assure that those willing to work are able to do so.

I have already mentioned the first difficulty standing in the way of adjustment in the labor market: the inflexibility of supply. If workers can do relatively little to reduce supply of labor when demand falls, can they do anything to stimulate demand? The answer to this question partly depends on the reason for unemployment, whether it results from inadequate accumulation of capital, inadequate aggregate demand, or competitive failure.

Unemployment bears a particularly frustrating relation to aggregate demand failure because in such cases unemployment acts as both cause and effect. To be unemployed is to be without income. To be without income is to be unable to purchase goods. When livelihood depends on exchange demand for goods depends on demand for labor. But demand for labor also depends on demand for goods because it is demand for goods that justifies hiring labor to produce those goods. This is the sense in which unemployment is both the cause and effect of demand failure. In order to stimulate demand for labor under conditions of demand failure, workers must stimulate demand for goods, and this is precisely what unemployment prevents them from doing.

Some suggest that the unemployed offer to work for less. If, however, they succeed in displacing those currently employed at higher wages, or force them to accept wage cuts, the overall level of demand for goods will fall due to the fall in the purchasing power of the employed labor force. When unemployment is due to aggregate demand failure, a wage cut exacerbates the problem rather than ameliorating it (see Kalecki 1969).

Under these conditions, workers desire more employment so they can purchase the goods firms desire to sell. But workers cannot buy those goods nor firms sell them. If the firms hired workers, they would in so doing create the demand for their own goods needed to make profit and justify the higher level of employment. Why do they fail to provide the employment and incomes needed to create demand for their goods?

In answering this question, we need to bear in mind the fact that firms make production and employment decisions individually, not collectively. Collectively, the employment offered by firms creates incomes used to buy the products those firms produce. But individually it does not. The income created when the individual firm offers employment is used primarily to buy goods from other firms. Thus no individual firm can solve its demand problem by, through increasing employment, creating incomes for its workers. Firms acting together could do so. But in a private enterprise economy, firms do not act together. As Adam Smith emphasized, each pursues its private interest with no concern for others. Any collective good results as the unintended consequence of the pursuit of private interest.

Because capitalist economy coordinates private decisions through the invisible hand of an unregulated market, the macroeconomic conditions needed to secure the well-being of the individual units are outside of their control. This becomes a problem because of economic interdependence. Because livelihood depends on exchange, decisions made by others determine our ability to acquire what we need. When those decisions lead to overall market failure, each agent suffers, although none can take action capable of altering the overall conditions. Indeed, the decisions that make sense for each unit tend to reinforce the adverse economic climate rather than relieving it. The fact that in market economies private decisions can have perverse effects points to an important limit of the market.

Will wage cuts raise the demand for labor when unemployment results from uncompetitiveness? Clearly, if differences in wages play an important part in the failure of firms to compete successfully, lower wages will improve their competitive position and, in so doing, encourage investment, output, and employment. Before recommending this cure, however, we need to be aware of some implications.

First, lower wages will not stimulate output and employment if competitive weakness results from attributes of the capital stock (such as its age and productivity), qualities of the product (such as reliability and performance), or management failure. Second, if wage differences are great enough, wage adjustments to improve competitive position mean significant change in living standards. This may be both politically and socially a price we cannot, or do not want to, pay.[3]

Political economy of the labor market

Unemployment highlights a key issue for political economy. In a capitalist economy, the wage simultaneously serves two separate, and sometimes inconsistent, functions. First, the wage is an important part of the firm's cost.

[3] I have not considered the problem of inflation and the role of the wage bargain (see Rowthorne 1980). Many economists argue that price stability requires unemployment and that the amount of unemployment needed to assure stability has risen over time. If we cannot have both price stability and (near) full employment, then making livelihood depend on exchange poses another serious problem. So long as we are not among the unemployed, unemployment may not seem such a high price to pay for stability. But surely for those unemployed or at risk, the price is high indeed.

As such, it affects profit margins and/or prices. Second, the wage is the price of labor and thus the laborer's income and primary source of livelihood. By making laboring capacity a commodity, capitalist economies make livelihood depend on exchange and link welfare to the cost structure of the economy.

This fact of life under capitalism creates a problem. The normal workings of the economy cannot guarantee that demand for labor will be adequate to provide livelihood for those whose primary asset is their labor. Further, the normal workings of the economy will not assure price stability, particularly in the face of shocks to the system such as that provided by oil price increases in the 1970s. When shocks of this kind lead to a spiral of wages and prices, the demands of livelihood confront those of profitability and stability.

One solution is for government to secure livelihood during those times when the market does not. Government provides a safety net of welfare services that, at least to a limited degree, assures income and well-being independently of the market. Since World War II, governments have also concerned themselves with measures aimed at supporting the level of demand during periods of recession.

Government could do much more than this. It could act as employer of last resort, guaranteeing employment and income where the market provides no such guarantee. When governments take steps of this kind, they, in effect, recognize that labor is not a commodity like others. While allowing the labor market to continue functioning, they do not accept it as the ultimate arbiter of welfare.

This seems reasonable enough, but it creates its own difficulties. By delinking welfare from exchange, governments undermine the ability of the market to assure that the wage, *viewed as a cost*, is consistent with the demands of profit making and price stability. This becomes particularly troublesome in an economy open to international competition. I consider some of these difficulties in Part IV.

The case of wages underscores the kind of trade-off we face in a capitalist economy. As we increase the role of the market in providing livelihood to citizens, we reduce the security those citizens experience in acquiring their livelihood. As we increase the role of government and reduce that of the market, we challenge the fundamental principle of a capitalist economy that livelihood depend on exchange. Doing so calls into question the arguments we use to justify the social arrangements that define capitalism.[4]

---

[4] These difficulties have been explored by Claus Offe (1984).

III

Inequality and difference

7

The classical argument for inequality

Differences between persons

Everything we have learned so far about a capitalist economy suggests that it fosters inequalities of income and wealth. Indeed, such inequalities follow directly from the basic principle of capitalism that income depends on property and thus livelihood on exchange. Each individual owns different property. Some own labor, some capital. Among those who labor, some get more in exchange for it than others. When we sell our capacities to acquire the money we need to satisfy our wants, our ability to satisfy our wants depends on the price we get. This price can vary dramatically, depending on the capacities we own and the market for them.

Markets value property according to the demand for it and, in this sense, its usefulness to others. Different individuals own different kinds of labor. A doctor's labor differs from that of a bricklayer, a professional athlete's from that of a cook, a stockbroker's from that of a teacher. What benefit do we gain from allowing these differences to form the basis for inequalities of income and wealth?

In our world inequalities require justification. This need to justify inequality stems from our underlying commitment to a notion of equality: that all persons should be treated equally, be afforded equal opportunity to develop and realize their capacities, and have their rights respected as private persons and as citizens. This assumption of equality makes inequality problematic. It does not exclude inequality, but it requires that inequalities be shown to be consistent with the underlying equality of persons.

Some are taller, some stronger, some faster. Some have musical talent while others are tone deaf. Some work hard while others have little motivation to work. How differences such as these translate into differences in income shapes our judgment of the inequalities that result from linking income to property. At least certain kinds of inequality are pernicious, and we need to know when income inequalities are of this type. These are the kinds of issues explored in this and the remaining chapters in this part of the book.

Differences in income stemming from differences in the market value of our capacities are important, but they are not the only or necessarily the most important differences bearing on income distribution. In addition to our capacities, we might own other assets capable of contributing to our income. People own different amounts and kinds of capital. When the price of oil is rising, those owning oil stocks benefit. During boom periods those owning real estate benefit; during the downswing they suffer. Differences in amount and type of nonlabor assets lead to different incomes for their owners.

The Reagan era, as one student observes, "was a heyday for unearned income as rents, dividends, capital gains and interest gained relative to wages and salaries" (Phillips 1990, p. 11). While those who lived off capital did very well – the head of Hewlett-Packard "found himself richer on paper by $1.2 billion" (p. 11) – those who depended on wages lost ground – "*[a]fter-tax* 1987 median family incomes were still well below those of the late 1970's" (p.15).

I begin with differences in income stemming from differences in capacities and then consider differences stemming from different kinds of assets, especially labor and capital. What sorts of factors affect the incomes different types of workers might expect to receive?

1. Education affects our capacities and, in general, a better educated person has more to sell and can get a better price. Economists think, perhaps perversely, of education as an investment on which the investor should expect a return. It involves incurring a cost to produce something – educated labor – that can later be sold at a price that should at least cover the cost. Sometimes it does; see Figure 7.1.[1]

2. Talent can affect our incomes given our education. Two persons with the same education might still have different abilities to do a job and therefore get different prices for their abilities.

3. Luck affects our income. We might win the lottery; or we might happen to be in the right place at the right time. We might own a house in a neighborhood where property values rise, or a stock that goes up. We might inherit money from relatives through no accomplishment of our own other than outliving them.

4. Hard work sometimes yields benefits. Many like to think that in a well-ordered economy it should do so, as that would provide a good reason for people to work hard. But, of course, people can work hard for other reasons

---

[1] For a fuller discussion, see Burtless (1990).

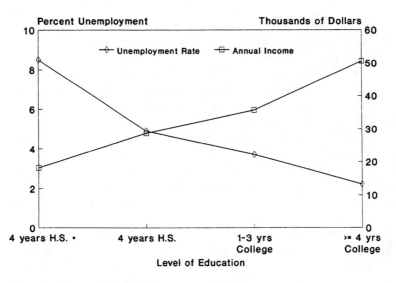

Figure 7.1. Education, employment, and income. *Source:* Statistical Abstract of the United States.

(they might have no choice in the matter), and hard work does not as a rule assure any reward. Most of those we consider poor work hard for their money. They are poor not because they do not work hard but because they do not get much for their work, whether or not they work hard and do it well.

5. Frugality is sometimes thought to bring the likelihood of a future improvement in income. The frugal save, and with their saving acquire capital, which provides a source of income. This source of income is potentially much more lucrative than labor. Those who own capital can expect considerably higher incomes than those who own little more than their capacity to labor. Whether you can save your way to ownership of sufficient capital to make a difference is debatable. But the idea that you could has inspired many advocates of private enterprise.

These five qualities are usually thought of as personal attributes. That is, they have to do with who we are individually and therefore what we can do and how well we can do it. It is a matter of vital importance to the argument for inequality that such qualities be understood in this way.

A different way of understanding them is as qualities we have because of groups to which we belong. What if the qualities that adhere to us because of group membership bear heavily on the value of our capacities in the market? What if women receive lower pay for their labor because they are women, or African-Americans because of their race?

If incomes vary according to group memberships of this type, they do not depend on our individual capacities and accomplishments. Such variation in incomes seem unjust precisely for this reason. Thus, a sixth factor can also determine difference in incomes:

6. Discrimination based on group membership rather than individual capacities often affects incomes in significant ways. We are discriminated against when we get paid less for doing the same work as others belonging to different groups or when we are prevented from developing our competence for a particular kind of job because of our gender, race, ethnic identity, or religion.

These are some of the main attributes people have that affect their incomes and wealth in a capitalist economy. The question about inequality is whether and why we should organize our economy to reward these qualities. In the following I explore some of the answers beginning in this chapter with the fifth item in the list.

Profit, inequality, and saving

In political economy, two sorts of justifications for inequality dominate, those centering on *incentives* and those centering on *rights*. If what we do affects our income and wealth, and if we wish to increase our income and wealth, inequality creates incentives for us to pursue those activities that yield greater remuneration. Thus inequality helps to allocate effort in particular directions, just as profit opportunities direct capital investments.

Regardless of incentives, we might consider certain inequalities inherently just. For example, if we think it only fair that income follow the ownership and use of property, then justice demands inequality. To get rid of such inequality, we would have to violate the principle linking income to property by redistributing the income gained by private persons through the sale and use of their property. I consider this argument in Chapter 9. Here, I explore further the incentive argument.

The incentive argument has many dimensions and comes in many forms. They all share a concern for the way inequalities direct persons to activities that yield social benefits, benefits not just for those who occupy positions of great income and wealth but also for those who do not.

In the classical version of the argument, inequalities mainly have to do with ownership of capital. If you own capital stock your income depends primarily on its profitability. If you do not own capital your income depends mainly on the market value of your capacities (your wage or salary).

In the classical theory, differences in income between capitalists and workers had important implications for investment and economic growth. Classical theorists tended to identify profit with saving and treat the difference in income between capitalists and workers as a way of mobilizing part of the national product for investment in additional capital stock. Income inequality was thus necessary to economic progress.

The classical argument expressed a broader idea with great importance in economics. For wealth to grow, productive capacity must increase. This productive capacity is lodged primarily in the capital stock. Thus the growth of the wealth of nations requires production of new capital stock – investment. This, in turn, meant that part of the nation's resources (especially labor) must be devoted to producing capital stock rather than consumption goods. Investment required the division of productive effort between that used to yield current consumption goods and that used to create the means to produce consumption goods in the future.

To grow, the nation must find a way to divide current income into two parts – investment and current consumption. The classical thinker found a solution to this problem in the organizational structure of capitalism. The capitalist system placed a large proportion of the national income (in the form of profit) into the hands of a small proportion of the population (the capitalists), who used it not primarily for their own consumption but to create more capital stock. The distribution of income was, in effect, a system of national saving and investment.

The classical economist emphasized the role of the capitalist who owned and operated a business firm with the object of making profit and accumulating capital. Today, we would be more inclined to emphasize the corporate organization than the individual capitalist, although individual capitalists continue to play the role envisioned for them by the classical economists. The business enterprise retains a part of its revenue (retained earnings) for the purpose of capital expansion. These retained earnings are what remains once the production costs are paid and the dividends distributed to stockholders. Retained earnings thus constitute saving. Thinking this way suggests that the division of output into investment and consumption follows from the organization of production around capitalist firms.

Subsequent to the classical period, the argument was generalized in a particular direction. In this generalization it is not only the inequality between capitalists and workers that leads to investment but also inequality of income regardless of its source.

To see this, assume that those with higher incomes tend to save a greater proportion of their incomes than those with lower incomes (the rich save more of their income than the poor). If the economy is divided into two groups, one with low incomes and one with high incomes – Group I and Group II – then the distribution of income between the two groups will affect the economy-wide amount of saving. Thus, if Group I saves 10 percent and Group II saves 40 percent, a shift in income from the former to the latter will increase saving:

Case A:	Group Income	Group Saving
Group I	$100,000	$ 10,000
Group II	$900,000	$360,000
Total saving will be $370,000.		

Case B:	Group Income	Group Saving
Group I	$400,000	$ 40,000
Group II	$600,000	$240,000
Total saving will be $280,000.		

The distribution of income is more unequal in Case A and the amount of group saving is correspondingly greater. When income distribution favors those likely to save more, Group II in both cases, social saving increases. A more egalitarian distribution of income reduces the overall level of saving.

If this idea is correct, and if saving leads to investment, then the greater the saving the greater the growth and progress of the nation. And if this follows, then the nation as a whole benefits from encouraging private saving out of income. Because saving enhances the assets of the saver and eventually his or her income, it furthers inequality.

This generalization of the classical argument runs into a difficulty, however. For capitalists, the object of saving is expansion of their capital, and the classical economists tended to assume that this meant the acquisition of new capital stock. Over the long run, this is not an unreasonable view of the nature of a capitalist economy. But when individuals save out of personal incomes, their purpose is not expansion of enterprise through increase in capital stock. Because of this, individual saving bears no immediate or necessary relation to investment in new equipment.[2]

For the economy as a whole, output is divided into consumption and investment goods. By definition, the latter equals social saving.[3] But individual decisions to divide personal incomes into saving and consumption do not add up in any simple way to determine social saving and consumption. Only when savings decisions mean purchase of new capital stock do they determine aggregate investment.

[2] This is one important element in Keynes's critique of the classical argument.
[3] Leaving aside government deficits and the trade balance.

The benefits of inequality

In the classical world as pictured here, inequality benefits everyone: It makes the nation richer; it increases the national capital; it leads to greater rates of growth and thus higher levels of employment. Higher levels of employment, in turn, lead to higher wage rates. Thus, to apply the criterion advanced by the philosopher John Rawls (1971), inequality under capitalism is justifiable because it benefits those with the lowest levels of income. Would you mind so much having an income significantly lower than someone else if (1) you had equal opportunity to acquire the higher income and (2) your lower income was, in any case, higher than it would be if incomes were equal?

Consider, for example, a choice between two economic systems, System A and System B, depicted in the following diagram.

	A	B
National income	$10,000,000	$24,000,000
Population	1000	1000
Income distribution	Equal distribution $10,000/person	Unequal distribution 50 people get $100,000 950 people get $20,000

If, in order to get to System B, inequality is necessary, as argued by the classical economists, your choice is between inequality of incomes where the lowest income is $24,000 and equality of incomes where the highest is $10,000. If you would choose B over A, and if inequality is indeed necessary to achieve B, you might well choose inequality over equality.

The classical argument supported the second of Rawls's conditions, that inequality benefit those receiving the least. Because of income inequality, a significant part of the national revenue is devoted to investment in new capital stock. The growth of the nation's producing capacity follows from saving and investment, which depend on inequality of distribution, especially that inequality linked to the distinction between profit income and wage income.

In the classical theory, the fundamental inequality of capitalist economy results from an inequality in the distribution of income-generating property. Because income depends on property, and different kinds of property yield different amounts of income, inequality of property ownership means inequality in the distribution of income. Of special importance is the inequality in the ownership of capital. Some receive the bulk of their income from the capital they own, but most receive the bulk of their income from the sale of their laboring capacity.

Those whose income comes from ownership of capital generally have the opportunity to obtain much higher levels of income than those who do not own capital and depend primarily or exclusively on wages. Those who own capital and receive profit have the capacity to use part of their income for the acquisition of new capital stock; they also have the motivation because it is through investment that their wealth expands. Growth of capital stock and thus of society's producing capacity follow from the concentration of capital ownership in the hands of a relatively small proportion of the population, the capitalists.

The fact that capitalists are motivated to invest in new capital means that they are motivated to save a significant part of their incomes. The fact that income from capital usually much exceeds its owner's consumption needs makes such saving possible. By placing riches in the hands of capitalists, society assures the growth of its capital stock. This growth benefits everyone (or most everyone) because it brings with it growth in productivity of labor and in the level of employment.

In its classical form, this argument focuses our attention on decisions made by individual capitalists about the use of their income from capital. In modern economies, much of profit income never accrues to individuals as their personal incomes but is retained by firms. And, of course, the individuals who receive income from capital ownership in the form of dividends do not spend it on new capital stock. Instead, firms do the work of the capitalists, seeking to expand their capital stocks, to improve the quality of their plant and equipment, and raise the productivity of labor. Firms thus also do the work of social saving needed to assure the future wealth of the nation. The link between the argument justifying profit on capital and that justifying channeling of profit to the legal owners of the capital (shares) may be a weak one.

The classical argument deals with inequality of income between persons who own different types of assets (capital and labor). It does not address the inequality of incomes between persons owning the same type of asset. Nor does it address the substantially higher levels of consumption afforded by income from capital, even when those receiving that income invest a large part of it.

What justifies differences in income between different types of workers and differences in consumption levels between workers and capitalists? The classical economists were not much concerned with this matter, but today it is an issue that has become difficult to ignore. We can attempt to extend the incentive argument to cover this case if we can claim that the higher levels of remuneration of some workers reflect their greater contributions to the wealth of society. In the next chapter I explore the strengths and weaknesses of this kind of argument.

Before turning to that aspect of the problem of inequality, I want to consider the first of the two assumptions listed earlier in support of the classical argument for inequality: that we each have equal opportunity to achieve a position that yields the higher rather than lower level of income. This assumption bears closer inspection. It expresses one of the most basic aspirations of a democratic society and confronts it with one of its greatest challenges.

Equal opportunity

Many have argued for a connection between the rise of capitalist economic organization and the spread of equality of opportunity, especially economic opportunity. Support for this claim is not hard to find. Ideally, markets are uninterested in people. They are interested instead in the commodities those people own and are prepared to sell. Markets care about commodities and not, for example, the race or gender of those who own them. One of the underlying principles of the market is that it concerns itself with the value of *what you own*, for example, how much money you have, rather than with *who you are*. Of course, in practice, the market falls short of this ideal. But, in principle, the ideal has great importance.

The market treats us as a bundle of capacities and assets whose worth has little to do with our social position or political power. Historically, the valuation of assets, including laboring capacity, independently of extraneous qualities has been a long and hard-fought accomplishment. It is, indeed, only in recent years that the goal of equal opportunity has been fully accepted in principle to apply to the opportunities for economic advancement of persons regardless of their social status, gender, race, or ethnic group.

> The term equal opportunity means that our life chances (including our chances to gain income and wealth) are not determined or significantly affected by our membership, formal or informal, in groups that we are placed into independently of our will. If you are treated differently because you are female in areas where gender is irrelevant to how you should be treated, then your membership in the female group significantly affects your life chances; you do not have equal opportunity.[4]

If we have equality of opportunity and yet end up with less wealth or lower income than others, we are more likely to view the difference as one of our own making and not one imposed on us by a society that relegates us to lower income because it defines us into a particular group.

---

[4] It is not always an easy matter to decide when gender is and is not relevant. The trend has been to interpret equal opportunity in a way that progressively narrows the relevance of gender considerations to a point where, in virtually all cases, it does not enter into consideration.

The idea that our situation (including our income) is of our own making is a vital one. Yet, knowing when we are responsible for ourselves is no easy matter. It is important to bear in mind that market institutions can only allow us to translate our talents and aspirations into income and wealth. They do not enable us to develop our capacities and make them marketable. Whether our situation is of our own making depends on what happens outside of the market: on our home experiences as they influence our character and the chance we have to develop our abilities, on the schools we attend and their ability to educate us, on the culture we experience and the value it places on the individual.

The market cannot assure that we bring to it all that we have the capacity for. If fairly organized, it can value our capacities on their own merits rather than on extraneous grounds (e.g. gender or race). But it cannot assure the development of human capacities. If we receive low value for what we have to sell, it may be because we have little potential or because we never had the opportunity to develop what potential we do have. In the first case the outcome is our own; in the second it is not.

This interpretation of equal opportunity, as relevant as it is, still begs an important question. If we have equal opportunity in this sense, does it follow that our accomplishments are therefore of our own making? The point of equal opportunity is to assure that we are responsible for ourselves. But it may not. Our opportunity may vary not with our race, gender, or ethnic identity but with the wealth and culture of our families.

Children born into families where reading is valued, whose parents read to them at an early age, have an advantage in the development of skills relevant to achievement in school over those who do not. Babies born into rich and poor households may not have equal opportunity even if they face no discrimination linked to attribution by others of a group membership carrying differential life chances. Or, put differently, family origin may be a kind of group membership that bestows differential rather than equal opportunity.

I return to the problem of poverty in Chapter 10. For the moment, it is important to bear in mind that the notion of equal opportunity is a vital one in justifying differences of income in modern societies. It is especially important to bear in mind that the modern justification for inequality hinges on making it the individual's responsibility so that it is not imposed on him but the result of his own decisions. This, then, raises the question: Under what conditions are we able to, and do we, make the crucial decisions that determine the trajectory of our lives as that affects our income and wealth?

An important implication for income distribution is sometimes drawn from the link between opportunity and responsibility. If our success or failure is out of our hands, this leaves us little incentive to work hard and strive to improve our situation. But if we think our fate is, to an important degree, in our hands, then we have an incentive to do those things likely to improve our condition. The more the market instills in us this sense of ourselves as masters of our fate, the more it creates incentives for us to work hard or in other ways be more productive. Thus the idea of opportunity is often linked to that of incentives. The claim is made that market institutions can help assure us control over the trajectory of our lives by placing vital decisions in our hands: how much to invest in what sort of education, what skills to develop, which occupation to pursue. This links the market to a kind of individual freedom often valued in modern societies.

In judging the market and its limits, however, we need to consider not only the opportunities it affords but also those it does not. Certain opportunities vital to our freedom cannot be provided by markets. The market depends on other institutions, such as those of the family and government, to assure that we have the capacities required to use it. When these other institutions fail, so must the market. A common reason institutions fail, however, is that they abdicate responsibilities to the market. In doing so they ask the market to accomplish ends it cannot. Asking the market to assure equal opportunity is an important example of failure resulting from inappropriate distribution of responsibilities across social institutions.

8

Income and productive contribution

Contribution equals remuneration

At the end of the previous chapter, I introduced the notion of equal opportunity and linked it to the idea that what we accomplish is up to us and not
imposed by group memberships over which we have no control. This idea
lays the groundwork for another argument in support of the fairness of the
inequalities implied in linking income to property ownership. This argument focuses on a connection between income and productive contribution.
If we can argue that our income equals our contribution, then we can be said
to take out what we put in. We might even go so far as to say that we get what
we deserve.

Getting what we deserve encourages us to feel that our economy has
distributed income fairly. But, more than this, it makes income distribution
an incentive system. If what we get varies with our productive contribution,
our desire to get more will lead us to try and contribute more. If working
harder, being more skillful or creative, or developing new more productive
methods will lead to a commensurate increase in our income, income acts as
an incentive to hard work, skill, and invention. If, however, we receive an
income independent of these attributes of our work effort, income does not
provide an incentive to increase or otherwise improve our effort. We may
find other reasons for working hard and being creative, but narrow self-
interest (in our material well-being) will not push us in that direction. In the
debate over capitalist economic organization, arguments for and against a
connection between income and productive contribution occupy a central
place. In this chapter I explore some of those arguments.

The neoclassical school of economics (see Caporaso and Levine 1992,
Chapter 4), which emerged at the end of the nineteenth century, emphasizes
a connection between the worker's productive contribution and remunera-

tion when markets are competitive. Let me briefly summarize this argument.[1]

Assume that production can go on with different numbers of workers and that there is a relationship between the number of workers and the level of output. Economists refer to this kind of relationship between inputs and output as a *production function*. A simple production function might be summarized in the following way:

Output	Labor input
10 units	1 unit(s) of labor
18	2
25	3
30	4
33	5

The production function as illustrated here exhibits what economists refer to as diminishing returns to scale.[2]

> *Diminishing returns to scale* refers to a relationship between additions of a productive input, in this case, labor, and additions to output that result from employment of the additional inputs. When the additional, or marginal, output falls as the amount of the input rises, that input is said to yield diminishing returns as the scale of production increases.

The assumption of diminishing returns to scale plays an important part in the argument that labor receives a wage equal to its productive contribution.

Diminishing returns makes most sense when we think about adding workers to a plot of land. As we increase the number of workers, we increase the output of the group of workers employed taken as a whole; that is, the output of the farm rises. But eventually the gains in output tail off as the additional workers have less and less useful tasks to perform.

Returning to the numerical example in the previous chart, assume that the price of the output is $1 per unit and the wage is $5 per unit (e.g., hour). Then we can rewrite our chart as follows:

Value of output	Labor cost	Profit
$10	$ 5	$ 5
18	10	8
25	15	10

[1] The classical treatment is Clark (1965). The argument was also applied to resources other than labor, such as land and capital. Doing so created significant problems. For a summary, see Harcourt (1972).
[2] For simplicity, I have left out the additional factors, in this case land. Strictly speaking, with land in the background, the example is one of diminishing returns to the labor factor.

$30	$20	$10
33	25	8

Note that the additional laborer's productive contribution can be compared to his wage of $5:

Labor unit	Productive contribution
First	$10
Second	8
Third	7
Fourth	5
Fifth	3

When the employer hires the first worker, he gets additional output worth $10 for a price of $5, the difference making up his profit. When he hires the second worker, he gains additional profit equal to the difference between that worker's productive contribution and his wage, in this case, $3. But when he hires the fifth worker, the difference between that worker's productive contribution and the cost to the employer is negative. The employer pays $5 to get $3.

An employer concerned with profit will hire workers only so long as their productive contribution at least equals their cost. Economists refer to the productive contribution in the last chart as the value of the marginal product, as it is the value of the additional (thus marginal) output (product) attributable to the employment of the additional worker. It is the loss in revenue that would result from laying off that worker.

It is in the employer's interest to add employees until the value of their marginal product or productive contribution equals the wage. If he hires fewer than this, he gives up profit he might make by employing more labor. If he hires workers beyond the point at which the wage equals the productive contribution, he loses money. This means, in effect, that in a competitive economy, where the employer can hire as many workers as he needs, the wage will equal the worker's productive contribution. In our example, the employer hires four workers and in so doing assures that the worker's remuneration ($5) equals his productive contribution.

The economist concludes from this that in a competitive economy the free market will tend to reward workers in accordance with their productive contributions. Thus we get what is owed us when we take back in income a value equal to what we have added to the product.

Our ability to think about the productive contribution of labor depends on our ability to associate parts of the product with individual units of labor. This can pose problems. The productive contribution must be, in some sense, the part of the product that exists because of what we have done, exactly that part that would not be there were we to withhold our effort.

Knowing our productive contribution, however, is no simple matter. Partly this is because we work together in producing and therefore cannot easily say that our productive contribution is our product. A worker on an automotive assembly line cannot be said to produce anything, at least not in any simple sense of the word. To be sure, he contributes to the production of the car, but he does not produce a car.

The division of labor implies interdependence of laborers, which makes it difficult to separate out their productive contributions. A more important difficulty, however, has to do with separating the productive contribution of labor from that of capital. In order to link productive contribution to remuneration, we must link the productive contributions of labor and of capital respectively to wages and profits. How do we know which part of the value produced by laborers working with capital equipment was produced by laborers, which part by their equipment? If we have no way of knowing, we cannot judge whether income corresponds to productive contribution. In the next section I explore this question further.

Productive contribution exceeds remuneration

When I made the assumption of diminishing returns, I did so with reference to an agricultural producer, a capitalist farm hiring wage labor. The picture was stylized even for agriculture. Now let us consider how the picture might look if the capitalist is a manufacturer and not a farmer.

A manufacturer owns capital stock. When he purchases his stock he acquires a certain amount of productive capacity. His output varies with the level of capacity utilization and depends on how much he thinks he can sell. The producer varies the level of capacity utilization by varying the amount of time he employs his machinery and the intensity with which he uses it. When the producer varies his output by varying the level of utilization of his capital stock, he varies the amount of employment he offers.

If, as he expands production and employs more labor, the additional workers are provided with machinery (e.g., looms for weaving sweaters, sewing machines for making shirts) equivalent to those already employed, then their productivity should equal that of currently employed labor. The addition to output resulting from employment of an additional unit of labor remains constant across a wide range of levels or scales of production. Many economists consider this situation the normal case, at least over a wide range of output levels in manufacturing. A typical production function is this:

Output	Labor input
10 units	1 unit(s) of labor
20	2
30	3

40 units   4 units
50   5

If the worker is paid a wage of $5 per unit of labor, and the price of output remains $1 per unit, then his productive contribution always exceeds his wage.

In this case the additional or marginal product of the worker has a value equal to the entire value of the additional units produced, or the price of the product. But this price also includes the profit of the producer made on the sale of the output produced:

$$Price = cost + profit$$

The worker's productive contribution equals his wage plus the remuneration of the capitalist.

Some economists, following the tradition of Karl Marx, would refer to this situation as the exploitation of labor. Exploitation refers to situations where workers produce more of the value of the output than they receive as wages. If the laborer's product includes the capitalist's profit, then profit making implies exploitation of labor. The income of one (the capitalist) was produced by another (the worker).

Under conditions where output increases in proportion to employment, the worker seems to produce both the profit and the wage. But even if there are diminishing returns, the worker can receive less than his product if his wage falls short of the additional product he contributes. When the wage is less than this additional product, we can say that the worker is exploited according to Marx's sense of the term.[3]

A debate over capitalism

The argument regarding productive contribution cuts two ways and has been central both in justifying capitalist economic organization and in criticizing it. Those who use it to justify capitalism do so by connecting productive contribution to remuneration. As we have seen, this raises some difficulties, and it cannot be said that in general a connection of this kind is very strong. Those who use an argument on productive contribution to criticize capitalism operate on the same ground as those who justify capitalism. They also require us to identify the worker's productive contribution in such a way as to allow us to compare it with his remuneration. This involves separating that contribution out as a distinguishable part of the value of the product. We must separate one worker's contribution from another's, as well as from the contribution of the non-labor inputs.

[3] This is not precisely the sense Marx had in mind. To understand Marx's idea more fully, we would need to discuss his theory of value and price. For a fuller and more precise discussion of Marx's theory, see Sweezy (1942).

The argument over productive contribution pits two powerful opponents against each other. On one side stands the theory favored by most economists according to which a free market economy tends to reward contribution. On the other side stands the claim that a capitalist economy takes the productive contribution of the many (workers) and transfers it to the few (the capitalists). Both sides require that we talk intelligently about the separable productive contributions of capital and labor.

We cannot just refer to profits and wages as if they measure productive contribution. Doing so rigs the contest because it makes productive contribution equal remuneration by definition. Neither can we assume (as Marx does) that all value is produced by labor (and is equal to the labor time expended) because that makes productive contribution unequal to reward by definition so long as profit is positive. We must, then, find a way of talking about (and measuring) productive contribution in a language other than that of profits and wages. And this way of speaking must not adopt as a premise what it is intended to demonstrate: that remuneration equals contribution or that profits are produced by workers. Thus far, economists have not had notable success in finding the right language.

Long-standing failures of this sort often reveal confusion in the original way of stating the problem – in this case as a problem about the relation between income and productive contribution. The difficulty is not just theoretical. Our experience of market economy leads us to think that we are paid for our contribution. But this does not mean that the amount we are paid equals the value of our contribution. That is, we know that if we produce nothing of value, we are unlikely to make any money (or hold our jobs very long). But this does not imply that what we are paid somehow equals the value we produce. Part of the reason for this has to do with the nature of modern production processes.

An important quality of the production process works against our efforts to know just how much the individual participant contributes. This quality is its integration.[4] Production is not a sum of separate efforts, but of a single, connected, process. Arguments for and against inequality that appeal to productive contribution ask us to think about the whole process as one that can be disassembled into a group of separate parts and, more significantly, of separable factors (labor and capital) working together, and not a collective process that takes away the separateness of the participants.

The arguments about productive contribution depend on an interpretation of the relation of the parts to the whole. They treat the system of production as something built up out of decisions and actions of individuals

---

[4] The implications of this quality of the production process for the argument that remuneration equals contribution are somewhat complicated. I outline them in the appendix to this chapter.

(capitalists and workers). The market puts together those decisions and actions to make the most efficient use of the prospective contributions (the capacities) of each. I think this idea has merit, but it also misses an important point.

Not only does a market put together the separate capacities and resources of individuals, it is the larger framework within which those capacities and resources take on meaning, including economic significance. In the next section of this chapter I explore what this means more concretely for the relation of government to the market.

Taxation

The idea that we can connect income to productive contribution suggests that our income is ours in a special sense. It only returns to us (in money) the value we have created. If, then, the government taxes our income, it takes something of ours away from us, to be used for purposes other than our own. The income tax feels this way. It is, after all, a part of our income that is taken from us.

But the discussion of remuneration and contribution raises an important question: In what sense is the income we receive ours? Have we earned it by producing something of equivalent value? If we cannot be said to have made a contribution equal in value to our income, has the government taken something of ours away when it taxes our income?

Our income is a claim that enables us to purchase a part of what we as a society produce. Those who think our income equals our productive contribution think our income gives us a claim over exactly what we produce. The claim is over specific goods we did not of course produce (auto workers do not just buy back the cars they produced with the income they received for producing them). But the claim is to a part of the product we can think of as equivalent (in value) to the goods we did produce. Because we think this way, we might oppose taxation as taking away from us something of ours and using it for purposes not our own. The "tax revolt" of the 1980s harbors an idea such as this.

If the argument linking contribution to remuneration fails, so does one basis for criticizing taxes on incomes. If remuneration does not equal contribution, then by taxing incomes the government does not reduce our claim over the national product below the level of our contribution. If we cannot know our individual part of the collective product, the claims of the collective may diminish, but they do not violate those of the individual. Indeed, if we view production as collective rather than individual, we are less likely to oppose government's use of output for collective rather than individual purposes.

How we think about taxes expresses the way we see ourselves connected to the larger community. When we assume that taxes take from us something that is ours, we understand our community to be something outside of us. That is, we think that the needs of community stand against those of the member. It is true, of course, that what we contribute to the collective product depends on our private attributes: industriousness, talent, ambition, skill, and so on. But what is our individual productive contribution without the larger framework of collective life? What would our contribution be worth without the infrastructure of roads, without the security provided by government, without the stability of the currency, without an educational system that seeks to produce an enlightened citizenry? All of this, and much more, comes to us from our collective body. By providing the infrastructure and framework, the community allows us to be productive and determines the value, if any, of what we produce.

This means that "our" product is both our own and that of the community to which we belong. It is our own in that we produced it by our effort, without which it would not exist. How much of it we have and how good it is depend on who we are and what we do. At the same time, our product is really that of the group to which we belong. The group makes it possible for us to produce, and the group values what we produce according to its contribution to the ends, however defined, of the political and economic system as a whole.

In a capitalist economy, this group valuation occurs in the market as a market determination of the price of our product and of the labor that went to producing it. The market value of what we produce depends on a large number of private decisions by others regarding what they produce or what they consume. These decisions determine the demand for our products, the costs of production, and the nature and intensity of competition from other suppliers. The market's evaluation translates private decisions into a collective result, a kind of implicitly collective decision regarding the worth of our efforts.

Even when the collective outcome results from private decisions, it always adds up to something more than those private decisions add up to taken each by themselves. The intermeshing of decisions and outcomes must assure that the system of mutual dependence of persons in production and consumption is secure. This system of mutual dependence is the something more that in a capitalist economy depends on the pursuit of private ends. In political economy we need to pay attention to this something more, to how it can be secured and the part played by both private and public decision making.

We must each decide to what we will devote our energies and talents. But we do not individually determine either the options available or what about us constitutes a talent. You can only have a talent for playing the violin in a world in whose history the violin has played its part. Your ability to run fast becomes a talent, indeed, a resource, in a culture of games centering on movement and speed. Whether your obsession with detail is a resource or a defect depends on the role of calculation and the value placed on accuracy in the larger culture. It may be up to us to develop and exploit our capacities and resources, but it is the collective culture and society that gives meaning and significance to those capacities and resources. Thus, they are ours, but not entirely. We depend on our communities to give meaning to what we accomplish individually. The costs of the community's upkeep are part of the costs of our own.

It is in this sense also that our output is both our own and that of the group. If we think of government as the steward of the collective body, the something more referred to earlier, then taxation appears in a different light. In this light, what the government appropriates for genuine collective ends, it also has a kind of right to. It redirects the collective product so that its use will serve not only the individual but the whole on which the individual depends. The government has a claim as meaningful as that of the private citizen. Because we produced our product together, we can also dispose of (at least a part of) it together.

When, as in a market economy, the collective product accrues to individuals as their private incomes, the government asserts the claim referred to earlier in part by taxing incomes. Because, in a private enterprise economy, the collective product is also so many private incomes, the collective use of the product removes it from private hands.

The emphasis we place on income taxes contributes to a way of thinking that understands government spending as a redirecting of private incomes to public uses. After all, we see the government's claim as a reduction from our gross income. The way our paychecks are written reinforces the idea that we are losing something. As our eyes scan our income statements, we see first the gross income, then a series of taxes taken away, then finally the net amount, usually substantially less than what we began with. Thus the form of the tax encourages a sense of having something taken away from us.

Avoiding this implication is one of the virtues of the so-called value added tax.[5] Unlike a sales tax, the value added tax is added not to the price of the good sold but to the difference between that price and the cost of the

---

[5] It also has some vices, the main one being the way it facilitates a regressive incidence of taxes. Like a sales tax, the value added tax, if applied uniformly, taxes those with large and small incomes at the same rate, where, at least in principle, income taxes can tax higher incomes at a higher rate. It turns out, of course, that income taxes have not been and are not very progressive (i.e., taxing higher incomes at a higher rate) and value added taxes can be arranged so as to tax the wealthy at higher rates.

materials purchased (in the case of retail trade to the wholesale price). For better and for worse, this removes payment of the tax from the consumer's experience. This is better because it works against the feeling that paying taxes takes something we had away from us (the something we had being, for example, the gross income on the left-hand side of our income statement). By so doing, the value added tax could contribute, in a small way, to rethinking our relation to government and especially the relation of our remuneration to the financing of government.

Appendix

One way to think about the productive contribution of an individual worker or a particular piece of capital equipment is to think about what would be lost of the aggregate (or national) product if that worker or piece of equipment were withdrawn. For example, the owner of the labor or equipment might decide he or she has some better use for it than as a productive input. The labor might be used as leisure. Used in this way, it yields no monetary income to its owner, but it does yield benefits that sometimes outweigh those money can be used to obtain. The piece of equipment, let us assume, can be used as a consumption good – perhaps I will use my tractor as a recreational vehicle. I know this all sounds a bit far-fetched, but there is a point to be made if we follow through to the end.

All we need do now is to calculate the value of output first when the labor or equipment is used as a productive input and then when it is not. Assuming the latter falls short of the former, we call the difference the productive contribution. We can now ask if it equals, falls short of, or exceeds the remuneration the owner of the input would have received for allowing it to be used productively.

Consider labor. Assume that both capital stock and labor supply are fully employed and that we remove a quantity of labor hours to be used for leisure rather than production. Output goes down by an amount that depends on productivity. In the first instance, however, the value of output lost does not equal the relevant productive contribution of the labor because (1) the capital stock is no longer fully employed, so we also lose some of its contribution, and (2) the materials that would have been used by the labor to produce output are not being used. When we lose some labor, we also lose the relevant contribution of the capital equipment and material inputs the labor would have worked with.

To get around this, we assume that when the labor hours are withdrawn, we can rearrange our capital stock so that we can fully employ it with the labor time remaining available. If we have less labor, we change the technique employed so that each laborer works with more equipment – we

increase the amount of capital per laborer. Economists refer to this as sub-
stitution. Only after this rearrangement has taken place (changed technique
and probably substituted some capital for labor) do we calculate the value of
output in the absence of the labor withdrawn.

This makes the calculation of productive contribution no easy matter.
What if the technology is not so flexible as to allow for the rearrangement
demanded for our calculation? If we cannot rearrange our inputs, then we
operate some at less than full capacity. Then the loss of some amount of
labor means loss of an amount of output that equals not the contribution of
the labor but the joint contribution of the labor, materials, and part of the
capital equipment now standing idle.

9

Rights and the market

Rights

The argument for distribution according to productive contribution suggests that we judge how incomes are distributed by comparing the actual distribution with an ideal state in which each receives an income equal to his contribution. A deviation from this state would be unfair. Thus, if the worker's contribution equals the sum of profits and wages (the whole net product), then the producer, in selling the good, acquires value to which the worker could make a claim. This is exploitation in the sense considered in the previous chapter. But a problem arises in making this judgment.

The employer hired the worker for a set amount agreed upon between them and explicitly written into their contract. Each party to the contract agreed to trade something he owned: one, money; the other, his or her laboring capacity. The property rights of each party were respected in the transaction. If we link the justness of income distribution to respect for the rights of the parties, the distribution resulting from voluntary contract is just whatever the relation is between it and productive contribution. Thus how we judge distribution depends on the criterion we use: productive contribution or respect for property right.

When we link distribution to productive contribution, we set up an ideal distribution we can use to determine if the actual distribution is fair or not. When our income falls short of our contribution, distribution deviates from the ideal. But when we judge distribution by whether property rights are respected, we do not refer to an ideal outcome but, rather, to a process. To paraphrase a contemporary philosopher, justice is a matter of how we arrive at the distribution of income and not how the configuration of that distribution compares to an ideal state (Nozick 1974). Justice depends on whether rights were respected in the process that placed goods into the hands of those who use and consume them.

I have spoken of productive contribution as reasonable grounds for judging distribution. In this chapter I ask: What right do you have to your income and wealth? As a part of this question, we can also ask, What right do you have to a remuneration equal to your productive contribution, especially if you entered into a contract that yielded an income less than that contribution?

> *Rights* are entitlements whose recognition is a substantial part of what it means for our personhood to be recognized. Respect for rights is, therefore, an important part of what it means to be a person. We exercise our rights when what we do depends on our will. This means that we do what we do at our own initiative. We are the source of, thus responsible for, our action; we decide for ourselves when and how we will act.

We have property rights over things when we use or dispose of them according to our own ends (at our will). We have rights in relation to other persons when our interaction with those persons is up to us and follows from our decisions. The key terms in understanding rights are initiative or agency and self-determination, autonomy, and freedom. Sometimes rights are linked to choice, and acting at our will is taken to mean making choices and acting on those choices. Rights allow choice, but they involve much more than choosing.

When we have rights, our sense of ourselves in the world differs from what it might be without rights or with only limited rights. This difference has to do with our capacity to see ourselves as centers of initiative. We see what we do emanating out of ourselves. In a somewhat different language, having rights means that we have the capacity for agency. This means that we act rather than being acted upon. Recognition of our rights allows us to be active, whereas the absence of rights can make us passive.

Consider the difference between welfare rights and charity. Charity depends on the generosity of others. It places the recipient in a subordinate and dependent position because the initiative rests with the giver. It denies the agency and autonomy of those in need. Welfare rights shift the balance. The recipient can, in principle, demand his or her rights. If welfare is a matter of right, then the initiative is on the side of the recipient. Because of this, in demanding welfare, the recipient need not be diminished as a person; he or she need not be made subordinate or dependent.

In practice, of course, the welfare system is notorious for creating dependence. There are several reasons for this, but among the most important is society's refusal to recognize welfare as a right. This refusal places those in need in a subordinate position that undermines their integrity and their sense of full and equal citizenship. We do this to those in need because of the ideas we have about them. One such idea explains the plight of the poor as the result of their lack of virtue. A variant on that idea suggests that humiliating the poor will encourage them to do what they must to get out of poverty. These ideas work against any recognition of welfare as a right because recognition of right maintains integrity and demands respect.

Examples of rights we do generally recognize include the right to own, use, and sell property, the right to privacy, and political rights such as the right to vote and the right to peaceable assembly. We have civil rights and sometimes economic rights, including those we associate with equal treatment in the job market.

Political economy is primarily concerned with two sorts of rights: property rights and economic rights. Property rights are the right to buy, sell, and use. They link things to persons (see Zucker 1993), making things an extension of the persons who own them and entitling their owners to dispose of them as they see fit.

Property exists within the domain or sphere of its owner as a kind of extension of his or her person. Thus, if someone steals my car or uses it without my permission, he has indirectly intruded on my person. The sense of violation that goes with being the victim of a theft suggests that more than material loss is involved. The feeling of violation results because property is an extension of self and the property relation a part of defining the space of the self.

Economic rights go beyond the rights that respect our disposal over our property.

> *Economic rights* are entitlements (to goods or money primarily) other than those we claim by claiming our property right: rights to work or to income whether we work or not, rights to welfare when we have no resources of our own.

A political economy can also contribute to the debate over economic rights. How extensive should they be? What implications does extension of economic rights have for the workings of the market system?

Our ability to exercise our rights depends on legislation protecting those rights. Prior to the appropriate legislation, women did not have the right to vote, and even their right to hold property in their own names was limited. Because the exercise of rights depends on legislation, some argue that legislation creates rights. Others argue that our rights are innate; laws protect them but do not create them. From this second standpoint, women had the right to vote before they were legally able to do so. The suffrage movement, then, demanded the recognition and protection of a right rather than its creation. We often claim to have rights that are not legally protected. Some claim rights for the handicapped and the unemployed as a way of arguing for the government to pass laws protecting those groups. Many have claimed that we have rights against the state, that we can in certain cases rightfully violate laws (Dworkin 1977).

When people are denied important rights (to vote or hold property) they are denied a part of what it means to be a person. Because they do not have full rights, those who do will not recognize them as fully persons. Thus wives were once seen as adjuncts of the persons of their husbands rather than as persons "in their own right." This situation places the oppressed group into a double bind because their status as less than full citizens is precisely the justification for their being treated as less than full citizens by being denied rights.

But it is only in the exercise of rights that we become fully persons, so to be denied rights is to be denied the opportunity to develop our personhood. To be granted rights does not simply establish the recognition of personhood, it sets in motion the development of the qualities we associate with fully being a person among persons. Rights are, then, both means and end.

Rights also develop. The meaning we attribute to our rights changes historically as does the extent of rights. These changes mean that the rights currently embodied in law do not stand as the last word on what are our rights. We can claim rights that are not legally recognized and try to gain legal status for them. When we make claims about rights that go beyond what is legally recognized and protected, what criteria can we appeal to? What sort of argument might make someone recognize the legitimacy of a right not currently protected by legislation? We can only answer this question if we know where our rights come from.

One way of thinking about where rights come from refers us to an ideal of personhood. If we have an ideal of how we think people should be treated by others and by their government, we can use that ideal to identify a set of rights that protect people from mistreatment. An important part of this ideal is a notion of personal integrity. Respect for rights helps to assure the integrity of persons. Violation of rights violates and undermines that integrity. We can, then, argue for a right by showing how it is needed to assure and protect personal integrity, especially in relations with others.

Integrity has two interrelated dimensions. First, it sets limits on the incursions of others (and of the state). It defines a boundary around the person, a space to which entry is possible only by invitation. Property rights and privacy rights are clearly justifiable on grounds such as this. Second, integrity refers to the wholeness of the person. It suggests an inner determination of action rather than one located outside. To have integrity is to determine yourself rather than following or even submitting to the ends of others. As I suggest further on, this sense of integrity has important implications for economic rights.

In claiming rights not currently part of law, we appeal to an idea we have of what is due to people in order to assure that they can determine their own actions, or act on their own initiative. Rights are connected to our ideas about self-determination. When we claim a right, we claim an area of action in which we expect to make the crucial decisions that affect our lives. Our rights assure that we can act as centers of initiative in the world.

The appeal to rights forms part of an ethical judgment or argument. By this, I mean an argument addressing not how we live and how our economy works but how we ought to live and how our economy ought to work. Ethical judgments concern what is possible and desirable. We can decide what is right or wrong, desirable or undesirable, in different ways. Asking what are our rights in the matter is one way of making such a judgment. Another might be to ask what arrangement will make us materially better off.

Economists since Adam Smith have tended to make ethical judgments on the basis of economic well-being. Economists ask what sort of economic arrangements will make us better off by making us more productive and efficient. But this is just one way of looking at the matter, and not necessarily the best in all cases. We can also ask what sort of economic organization best assures that our rights will be protected. And, depending on what rights we have in mind, this can lead in a different direction than asking about productivity or efficiency.

This distinction among criteria for making ethical judgments parallels the distinction between incentives and rights in judging income distribution. Do we judge income distribution by how well it provides incentives for productivity and efficiency, or do we judge it by how well it respects rights? How we choose to proceed can make considerable difference. In previous chapters I considered the role of incentives. Here I consider the way our economic arrangements might look from a rights-based vantage point. If we approach the problem of inequality in the distribution of income and wealth on the basis of rights, how would we judge the inequalities implied in capitalist economic organization?[1]

The property rights argument

One answer makes respect for property rights do all the work. If we focus our attention exclusively on property rights, then, in thinking about distribution, we need only concern ourselves with whether property is in the hands of its rightful owner. Whether it is or not can be judged by asking how the current holder of the property acquired it. If it was acquired with due respect for the property rights of others, then it is rightfully held. Acquisition of property with due respect for the rights of others means:

[1] For a fuller discussion, see Caporaso and Levine (1992, Chapter 9), Levine (1988), Winfield (1988), and Zucker (1993a).

1. Acquisition through exchange from its rightful owner who freely agrees to sell it
2. Acquisition of a gift, freely given by its owner
3. Appropriation of something owned by no one, and whose acquisition does not adversely affect the situation of others

We can use this simple rights-based approach to evaluate whether the distribution of income in a capitalist economy is ethically justified. To do so, we must first judge the (historically) original acquisition of the property currently owned by individuals and firms. Practically speaking, this is no easy matter. If, for example, the property in question was originally acquired by force (perhaps from the Native Americans who were by treaty its rightful owners), then subsequent transactions by which the property changed hands were, in effect, the transfer of stolen property and not valid contracts. The requirements of a rights-based distribution can be extremely stringent in demanding redress of past wrongs. Leaving this difficulty aside (admitting that it is a real and serious one), the problem of judging distribution becomes relatively simple.

If the worker freely enters the wage contract, then so long as he or she is paid the amount stipulated in the contract, the resulting distribution is just. In arriving at this conclusion, neither productive contribution nor the impact of the arrangement on the growth of national wealth matters.

Income from the use and ownership of capital – profit – accrues to the owners of property who by right can use it as they wish, including to make themselves wealthy. So long as they violate no rights of others in using their property, the income they (or by extension their property) generate is theirs.

The basic principle employed is something like the following: What you do with your property is your business and yours alone. The only limitation recognized on the use of property is that you do not use it to violate the rights of others and that it is, in fact, yours. The distribution of income is the result of a large number of private decisions made by property owners regarding how they will employ their property (including their laboring capacity).

Understood in this way, your income is yours not because you earned it but because you used or exchanged something you owned to get it. If you become rich by saving, hard work, skill, or good fortune, you use your property to create wealth for yourself, and this wealth is rightfully yours. If you are poor because of ill fortune, prodigality, lack of talent, or laziness, your poverty is also yours. Your poverty has to do not with what others do, and do to you, but with who you are and what you do to yourself.

The conclusion in the last paragraph is important. This property rights-based vision sees the distribution of income as a reflection of attributes and actions that express the inner resources, drives, ambitions, desires, and capacities of individuals. We do not get what we contribute, or even necessarily what we have earned, but we do get what is ours.

This is in some ways an appealing conclusion. But before fully embracing it, we need to consider the limits of property rights more closely. Can we exclude the possibility that what we get in a world governed by property rights (be it wealth or poverty) is in important ways imposed on us? If you are poor in such a world, is your poverty yours and not something imposed on you either by others or by the economic system as a whole? Of special importance, does the pursuit of wealth by some exclude the acquisition of wealth by others? Karl Marx argued that it is the activity by which some become rich that makes, or at least keeps, others poor.

The idea of exploitation introduced in the previous chapter suggests that how we fare depends more on what others do than on what we do. Exploitation denies that we are the agents of our lives. For Marx, the profit received by the capitalist as his income was produced by the laborer. If this is so, and profit making makes us wealthy and earning a wage does not, then the wealth of the capitalist comes at the expense of the worker.

If Marx is correct in viewing profit as the worker's product, it means that when some exercise their property right by using their property as capital to accumulate wealth, they thereby make others poor, or at least prevent them from improving their condition. In some way this exercise of right prevents others from providing themselves an adequate livelihood. This is an important question in political economy. We cannot resolve it here, but we can explore some of its more important dimensions.

Externalities and coercion

Are my capacities and limitations, the opportunities available to me and those beyond my reach, really my own, or are they imposed on me by circumstances outside my control? In the following chapters I explore different dimensions of this question. For the present I want to summarize the key general issues. They are two:

1. Do the legally voluntary transactions that distribute income in a capitalist economy contain a significant element of coercion?
2. Do those transactions implicate non-participants in ways that affect their well-being and are thus relevant to our judgement of the distribution of income that results?

I will elaborate briefly on these two issues.

When we participate in markets, what we do affects others. It contributes to their welfare by providing opportunities they might not otherwise have. We offer them the chance to improve their well-being by participating in a mutually beneficial trade. Because we do not force them to participate, we must instead entice or induce them. The inducement is the prospect that the trade will make them better off than they would be if they held onto their original property. Because they are (legally) free not to trade, doing so means that they think the trade makes them better off. If we trust their judgment of themselves and exclude coercion, voluntary transactions must enhance their welfare.

Of course, this enhancement of well-being is relative. It is relative to circumstances prior to exchange. After the trade, we are better off than we would be had we held onto our original property. But what if we have little property to begin with? If we have no property but our laboring capacity, then we must trade it for the money we need to buy the means for sustaining ourselves. For those with little or no property other than laboring capacity, livelihood depends on exchange, and because of this, the opportunities afforded by the market may be relatively narrow.

The greater our resources, including the value of our laboring capacity, the richer our opportunities. Our talents and skills have a worth we can translate into income and wealth. The greater the income and wealth we can acquire, the wider our set of opportunities. The outcome depends on the way the market system values our property and the amount we happen to have.

Economists often claim that legally voluntary transactions improve the welfare of participants. Why make an exchange you think will leave you worse off? This claim about welfare improvement following voluntary trade holds our attention better the more real our choices. What is legally voluntary may not be substantively so. Economists sometimes confuse the two. Even if by law no one can force me to sell my labor to a fast-food restaurant, if I have no other source of income and if my labor has a very low market value, I may have no choice. The same may hold to a greater or lesser degree for most unskilled labor. This transfers the question of how voluntary a transaction is onto the question of access to skills and the reasons some have them and others do not. Knowing these reasons bears on government policy directed at improving citizens' life prospects.

Another example has importance in less developed economies. Consider an economy based on small-scale agriculture undertaken by (peasant) farmers who own or have rights to the land they work. If these peasants can acquire needed productive inputs (e.g., seeds or equipment) only by borrowing the money to buy them, then they must be able to realize sufficient income from selling their output to pay the service on their debts. These peasants enter into commerce in order to repay debt because their incomes are too low for them to afford to purchase the productive inputs they need.

While their market activities are legally voluntary, they have no choice. What is legally voluntary may also be forced (see Bhaduri 1986).

Transactions, even if legally voluntary, often affect people not party to them. Economists refer to these effects as externalities.

> *Externalities* are effects of market transactions on the well-being of individuals not party to those transactions.

Smoking cigarettes in the presence of nonsmokers lowers their welfare and imposes costs on them they did not voluntarily incur. Building a house that blocks the view from a neighbor's window (or even painting your house a color your neighbor abhors) imposes a cost and lowers well-being. Driving a car that pollutes the air or flushing pollutants into a stream used for recreational purposes adversely affects the well-being of others not party to the transactions and decisions that led to the acts that polluted the air and water. These are examples of externalities.

Unemployment can also be viewed as an externality. When low rates of investment inhibit the demand for goods, firms respond by decreasing their scale of production; the result can be unemployment. The unemployed workers suffer from effects of decisions made by others.

When contracts affect those not party to them, we need more complicated criteria for judging the fairness of distribution than whether the rights of the parties are respected. We need to consider the wider context of interdependence and how the contract impinges on many others, even a whole community, if we are to judge the fairness of the distribution of income that results.

Externalities result from the interdependence of individuals in a market economy and thus from the fact that what they do with their property has widespread effects. We live and work together. We depend on others for the things we need to sustain our ways of life. We produce for each other.

The property rights argument summarized in this chapter refers us to a vision of a world of separate, independent property owners interacting only when they choose to do so and choosing the interactions that affect them. This vision minimizes interdependence. Ideally, it makes us depend on others only when we choose to and when it is in our interest to involve ourselves with them. We are not forced into interaction by the demands of neediness. It is not that we must but that we choose. The discretion we have because we are not required even by our own need to interrelate with others allows us to evaluate transactions exclusively by looking at the property rights exercised in them. Because we are independent in our actions from ends and outcomes imposed on us by others, those outcomes are our own. We make them what they are. But if we cannot exclude the "must" from our relations with others, respect for property rights in those relations tells only part of the story.

In an interdependent world, the issues of autonomy and coercion and of uninvited imposition of effects of transactions cannot be ignored. A simple property rights argument will not suffice for evaluating economic arrangements. In considering the individual transaction, we must place it in the context of a larger community.

In thinking about the inequalities built into a capitalist economy, we are forced to consider what it means for our life situation to be of our own doing, for our accomplishments to be ours, and for the transactions we enter into to be voluntary and welfare improving. How can we judge the responsibility of the individual for his or her situation and, in this sense, the justness of the placement of that individual into that situation (whether it be one of wealth or of poverty)? One of the important claims of a market-centered society is that it allows for, even insists on, individual responsibility while encouraging individual achievement. But individual responsibility and achievement are no simple matters.

Economic rights

Up to this point, I have considered a rights-based approach centered exclusively on property rights. In defining rights, however, I included the possibility that rights other than those protecting property might bear on distribution. I referred to these other rights as economic rights and suggested a connection with personal integrity. Economic rights are aimed at protecting and assuring wholeness.

In speaking of wholeness, I had in mind our sense of ourselves as capable of acting on our own initiative. I contrasted this way of being in the world with those we might describe as passive, submissive, and compliant. One of the mainsprings of the passive or compliant attitude is dependence stemming from an inability to manage for oneself. To be independent we must have some basic competencies: literacy, physical health, the ability to make our way in the day-to-day world. Independence also demands intellectual competencies that include knowledge, intelligence, and relevant job skills, and personal competencies such as the capacity to take responsibility for our actions (e.g., to show up at work on time) and the inner confidence that we can learn to do a job we have not done before. Without competence, respect for rights will not translate into the ability to make a living that exploits our potential.

The entitlements I refer to as economic rights aim at assuring that we can develop and exercise these competencies. Economic rights go beyond property rights by speaking to the conditions we must satisfy if property rights are to have meaning and work for us. To exercise our rights in a meaningful way, we must have the competence to act on our own initiative.

If we cannot afford adequate health care, our physical capacities may deteriorate. If they do, we can lose some or much of our ability to work and to gain the income and satisfaction provided by work. Our opportunities diminish. If we cannot afford education, or if a handicap implies special educational needs, we are unlikely to be able to make our way by ourselves. The market becomes obstacle rather than opportunity. If our home life deprives us of the parental care and concern needed to develop a robust sense of ourselves, of our capacities and prospects, we may fail to take advantage of what is offered by the property system. Such failure is ours in a sense. It is not imposed by the property system except in a negative sense, the sense in which negligence imposes damage.

The negligence of the property system is one of its most important qualities. Understanding where it is negligent helps us understand what we must provide through nonmarket means. The term economic rights refers us to some of the areas of market negligence and governmental responsibility.

Rights create opportunities. When our rights are respected, what we do is up to us. Therefore, what we accomplish is also up to us. We have the opportunity to see what we can do. Although rights create opportunities, they do not determine whether we take advantage of those opportunities and what success, if any, we achieve. A society organized to respect individual rights allows some to fail. If failure leads to destitution, as it might in a capitalist society, government can lend support to protect basic humanness so far as possible and to revive opportunity so that the individual might try again. Government does not guarantee success. Our right is to pursue happiness, not to be happy.

The right is to pursue happiness rather than be happy because our happiness must be of our own making. The assumption here is that real happiness stems from accomplishment, the sense that what we have become we have made of ourselves. Such an assumption does not exclude dependence on others, but it does exclude the kind of dependence that allows others to take responsibility for us.

If we think of the economy as a set of opportunities, then government can help make those opportunities real for each of us so far as possible. How far it is possible depends on our talents and interests. The government cannot stand in for talent and interest, giving us the satisfaction of exercising talents we do not have or pursuing interests not our own. The government's concern remains primarily opportunity rather than outcome. Economic rights extend our opportunities in important directions. A market economy provides a set of opportunities, but it cannot open up its opportunities to all;

some need assistance if the opportunities of the market are to open up for them.

But economic rights sometimes point beyond opportunity. A government retraining program provides for those whose opportunities may be shrinking to a point that endangers their integrity; a government guarantee of an income without regard to work assures an outcome. To guarantee incomes independently of work actually removes one opportunity from the market – the opportunity to acquire income according to talent, hard work, and good fortune. Society can decide that some opportunities should not be provided because they threaten important values or other rights considered more basic.

Employment guarantees lie somewhere between a guarantee of income and the free market outcome. For government to recognize a right to a job, it must act as employer of last resort. When no private sector employment is available, each citizen could turn to government and demand a job. By acting as employer of last resort, the government would assure an opportunity vital to well-being in capitalist economy, the opportunity to acquire an income. It would also assure an outcome, the acquisition of a job.

Because of the two-sided nature of employment rights, they generate considerable controversy. Historically, the United States has not recognized a right to a job largely on the grounds that it removes an opportunity needed to make the capitalist system work well: It undermines the link between income and work and thus weakens the work incentive built into a capitalist economy. Weakening the work incentive is thought by some, correctly or not, to have potentially dire consequences.

The prospect of dire consequences, of course, is acceptable only when the economy performs well. If the economy works poorly in providing jobs to those who want them and are willing to work, it challenges its own argument against a right to a job.

Equality and efficiency

Property rights encourage inequalities between persons, whereas other economic rights tend to foster greater equality. The broader our interpretation of property rights, the less we can inhibit the tendency for wealth holders to use their property to enhance their wealth and income. Those who interpret income taxes as a violation of property right employ such a broad interpretation. They argue against measures that would provide all citizens access to an amount of wealth adequate to maintain a minimum standard of living. To provide such a minimum – including, presumably, adequate health care, education, housing, food – requires that we reallocate resources to the needy.

One conclusion economists draw is that extension of rights beyond the right to hold and use private property increases equality at the expense of efficiency (see Okun 1975). They draw this conclusion by appealing to the incentive argument. The more equal the distribution of goods and services, the less the incentive for some to use their skills and talents to enhance efficiency and productivity. The more equal the distribution of output, the less the reward to those whose effort and ingenuity we call upon in producing it.

If this is the case, there must be a conflict – in the economist's language, a trade-off – between the goals of equality and efficiency. The more we provide goods and services as a matter of right rather than ability to pay, the fewer goods and services we are likely to have available. In concluding my discussion of rights and the market, I will briefly explore this argument (see Schelling 1984, Levine 1983b).

The idea of trade-offs motivates much thinking in economics. Whenever we employ our resources in one direction, we deny their use for alternative ends. Spending so much of our labor and capital to build a hospital means we cannot use that labor and capital to build auto factories or ice-cream parlors. If providing medical care as a matter of right increases the amount of medical care we use, it thereby reduces resources available to satisfy other wants. It also reduces what is available to reward industriousness, thrift, and innovation.

This might not be the case. If our economy operates at less than full capacity, leaving labor unemployed and capital stock unused, providing more medical care need not diminish the amount of other goods and services available. The trade-off argument presumes, then, that we are operating near capacity so that increasing entitlements must redirect resources; something must be lost. We need to bear this limitation of the trade-off argument in mind because capitalist economies rarely operate at full capacity.

Still, I do not think matters of level of capacity utilization make the trade-off argument irrelevant. Operating at less than full capacity is a problem in itself. Were it solved, we would then need to think about alternate uses of our resources and accept that providing more medical care or housing means providing less of something else. If the something more we provide is provided to everyone as an entitlement, increasing the proportion of output devoted to it reduces the amount remaining to subsidize the inequalities we associate with economic incentives. Does this mean that at full employment the trade-off between equality and efficiency kicks in? I think it may, but not to the extent often assumed.

Some important difficulties remain to be considered. First, the argument assumes that the relation between reward and contribution is a kind of

continuous function: The greater the reward, the greater the payoff in productivity and efficiency gains; the less the reward, the slower economic
growth and growth in productivity. If such a functional relation existed, then
each time we increased entitlements by a given amount, we would reduce
economic growth or productivity gain by some corresponding amount (the
proportions depending on the specific form of the function).

But, of course, incentives need not work that way. It might be enough that
we provide meaningful incentives to those who work hard or innovate, but
not very important how much those incentives are. When President George
Bush visited Japan with a group of U.S. auto company executives, the trip
proved embarrassing in part because it highlighted how much lower salaries
are for top executives in Japan (where their efforts have provided substantial
economic benefits) than they are in the United States (where the payoff for
those particular incentives is hard to find).

The possibility that the amount of the payoff may be less critical than we
have come to believe has relevance for a currently popular proposal for
stimulating economic growth: reducing the capital gains tax. Entirely apart
from the likely incentive reducing capital gains taxes might have for (unproductive and potentially harmful) speculative activities in real estate and the
stock market, the argument runs up against the difficulty that it assumes a
marginal increase in the payoff to holding capital matters to those engaged
in capital investment. If it does not, we can secure the cooperation of entrepreneurs without giving up tax revenues we might use to expand entitlement
programs.

Finally, consider more closely the way of thinking embedded in the trade-
off argument. It treats entitlement as the negative of incentive. Doing so
ignores two important implications of entitlements. First, entitlements can
act as incentives. Second, providing entitlements can reduce costs by changing the criteria used to determine expenditures.

Providing entitlements assures that, so far as possible, all citizens can
secure their capacities for participation and productive contribution. Adequate health care and education enable many otherwise excluded to make
meaningful contributions. To assume that doing so reduces the size of the
overall pool of goods and services ignores the contributions lost due to the
significant disincentives life in poverty creates.

Entitlements can draw otherwise marginalized sectors of the population
into productive work. By dispelling hopelessness and alienation, entitlements can enhance rather than diminish productivity.

While we tend to assume that providing entitlements increases costs and
the "burden of government," this is not always the case. To see the limitations in this assumption, it helps to recall the distinction between wants and
needs. Thinking in terms of trade-offs amalgamates all our ends under the

heading of wants. But all of our ends are not alike. Some involve choices we need to make based on how we think a particular good or service will contribute to our level of satisfaction. Others involve demands imposed on us in ways that deny the relevance of calculations and trade-offs among ends.

The second category, needs, includes such things as education and health care. If entitled to these goods, the amount we consume will depend on the amount we need. Equality of health care means not that all receive the same care but that all receive the care they need. Granting thorny issues concerning heroic and experimental treatment, the possibility that we might consume as much as we need does not imply that we will consume more than we would under the rule of the free market.

When health care depends on income, we acquire not the amount we need but the amount we want and can afford. For the rich, this can be considerably more than they need, whereas for the poor it is often considerably less. Inequalities in wealth of sufficient magnitude provide for some the opportunity to use the nation's resources to acquire expensive and unnecessary care. Those without the income to afford adequate care often become costly burdens. The most notorious example of this is prenatal care. Inadequate prenatal care endangers the health of infants and sometimes results in later medical problems that cost substantially more than prenatal care.

In cases of need, expansion of entitlements may not be costly and may not erode incentives for hard work and innovation. Yet failure to provide entitlements can adversely affect incentives and significantly increase costs.

10

Poverty and inequality

Poverty

Capitalism holds out the promise of economic well-being for those who immerse themselves in the market, the "cash nexus" as Marx refers to it. Admission to the market is open to anyone with something to sell. By the same token, however, the market is closed to those with nothing of (market) value. The market is the ultimate arbiter of who has something of value and how much that something is worth.

The market has no interest in assuring that we all have something of value or that the value of what we own will be sufficient to provide us income adequate to meet our needs. The possibility always exists that we will be left out. If we are left out, then the private enterprise economy tells us that we must bear the burden of the worthlessness of our endowment. Those left in this state are the poor, and their state is one of poverty (see Dreze and Sen 1989).

Poverty means deprivation, but deprivation of what? Poverty means unsatisfied wants, but wants of what kind? Before exploring the relation of poverty to capitalism, we need to consider further what it means to be poor.

Clearly, we could take survival as a benchmark, perhaps treating famine as the limiting point of poverty. Yet famine differs from poverty in that, unlike famine, poverty is a way of life. Understanding poverty as a way of life demands that we define it in broader terms than those suggested by the notion of survival. Poverty threatens survival in a number of ways. Poor nutrition, inadequate sanitation, and social disintegration all make life uncertain. But your ability to survive hardly implies that you are not poor.

In searching for a benchmark we can use to identify poverty, the notion of subsistence introduced in Chapter 2 might prove relevant. Falling below subsistence deprives us of our normally expected (because previously attained) way of life. It means wants go unsatisfied. Does this make us poor?

114

Certainly, the failure to achieve subsistence carries some of the dimensions of poverty. However, it seems to miss others.

Particularly worrisome is the fact that we define subsistence in relation to an expectable level of living. An investment banker who loses his job on Wall Street and goes to work as middle management in a bank in Scranton must give up an established way of life. In a way, he or she is impoverished; but this is not what we mean by poverty. We still lack the more general standard that the term poverty suggests.

The concept of opportunity might help (see Sen 1987, p. 37). The way of life we are able to attain given our income determines what opportunity we have to pursue life projects and gain satisfaction from the development and utilization of our talents. This suggests a definition of poverty:

> *Poverty* means deprivation of opportunity.

The connection between opportunity and income (or wealth) in a capitalist society suggests a further elaboration of this definition:

> *Poverty* means income below a level that would sustain a physical and emotional life allowing the individual to take advantage of the opportunities available given his or her talents and interests.

The notion of available opportunities needs some clarification. Unless we can pin down the kind of opportunity whose availability assures that we will not be poor, our definition remains incomplete.

Our earlier discussion of the use of wealth helps. There I emphasized the use of wealth to assure esteem, autonomy, and security. Each of these in turn contributes to our ability to make our lives our own. That is, these uses of wealth sustain individual freedom. Thus the opportunity that a measure of wealth affords is the opportunity to live a life informed by self-determination and the regard of others in a secure environment. Poverty means deprivation of this opportunity.

This definition will not easily translate into a dollar figure, and we could debate what sort of income allows opportunity. But, given some agreement on the vital dimensions of opportunity – education, physical and emotional well-being, access to cultural opportunities – we could estimate the needed level of income and standard of living.

Our definition of poverty has an interesting implication. The positive side of capitalist development is its ability to expand opportunities by expanding wealth. This has meant historically that the meaning of opportunity has also expanded. Our notions of education, of physical and emotional well-being, and of culture have changed in ways that carry an increasing price tag. As they change, so must the level of income that defines the line between those who are poor and those who are not. In addressing the problem of poverty

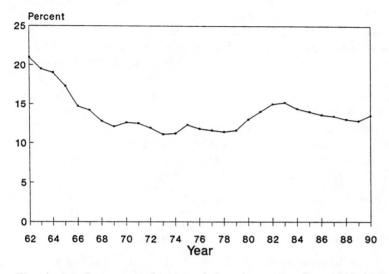

Figure 10.1. Percentage of persons below the poverty line, 1962–1990. *Source:* Statistical Abstract of the United States, 1975, 1982–83, 1992.

we return, then, to two underlying concerns about capitalism: (1) What is the relation of capitalism to opportunity? (2) When does capitalism assure income adequate to prevent our falling below the line that defines poverty?

When the U.S. government calculates poverty, it begins with what it calls the poverty line or minimum family income needs (see Sawhill 1988). This level is calculated by taking the cost of a "nutritionally adequate diet" and multiplying by three. The calculation assumes that the normal family spends approximately one third of its income on food (based on survey research done in the 1950s). Poverty levels since 1966 are charted in Figure 10.1.

The poverty line for a family of four in 1990 was $13,359. By this criterion of what is poverty, a family of four with an income greater than $13,359 was not poor. Even given this level of living, 33.6 million people (13.5 percent of the population) were poor in 1990.

Considering what could be had in 1990 for $13,359, we can wonder whether those above that level really had escaped poverty. Did this amount of money support a way of life likely to assure esteem (particularly self-esteem), autonomy, and security? Does this level of income afford the material means to take advantage of opportunities made available in a modern society? Could the children in the family afford to attend college? Could the parents afford to provide the means for the cultural life and development of the family? Was adequate medical care available? Could clothing be purchased that allowed family members to gain acceptance in their peer groups?

Questions like these have to do with income levels that afford an adequate way of life and not the minimum nutritional needs for survival.

It is often thought that we are better off for having our nutritional needs fully met and that we owe this to the development of market institutions. In Chapter 1 I suggest why this might not be an accurate assessment of the human condition. Recall Marshall Sahlins's description of life in what he terms the "primitive affluent society."

The wealth brought us by the institutions of market economy introduces us to a way of life unavailable to primitive cultures, offering us new opportunities. What we need to understand is that our institutions bring us the opportunity for both wealth (the new way of life) and poverty (failure to achieve that new way of life).

If we have little more than our basic subsistence needs met in a market economy, then that market economy has not done well by us. It has not provided us with the new way of life afforded by the amount and kind of wealth produced under capitalism. And, in 1990, 33.6 million people in the United States did not have even that much to show for life under capitalism.

Some economists use facts like these to build an indictment of capitalism. If capitalism excludes large numbers of people from participation in what Adam Smith referred to as "civilized society," and if its benefits are limited, then we may want to reconsider our enthusiasm for it.

In doing so, a useful question to ask is one alluded to at the end of the last chapter: Does capitalism make people poor, or are they poor because of their own failings? Who is responsible for poverty? Our answer could bear on what we think ought to be done about the fact that large numbers of people remain poor.

The poor

Those left out under capitalism generally fall into two groups: the working poor and the unemployed (or underemployed). The working poor are those who, while employed more or less full time, do not receive income adequate to sustain a way of life that would take them out of poverty. The unemployed and underemployed include those who have lost their jobs due to the state of the economy and those who are unable to find employment due to the lack of market demand for whatever skills they may have (they may have few or none). The first group is poor because their one asset, labor, does not have an adequate market value. The second group is poor either because there is no demand for their asset or because they have none to sell. In this connection it is worth remarking that more than 40 percent of the poor work full time (Ellwood 1988, p. 89).

We cannot give a single answer to the question who is responsible for poverty, for poverty comes in different forms and occurs for different reasons. Let me flesh out the groupings indicated earlier.

1. Poverty results from low wages for those who work more or less full time. These are the working poor. Their poverty results from the low market value of their capacities.
2. Poverty results from unemployment due to lack of adequate demand for labor. This can also be subdivided into two cases:
   (a) Long-term unemployment due to changes in the market structure, such as movement of industry to other regions or countries. When demand shifts to automobiles imported from Japan, the U.S. auto industry experiences a long-term decline in its market share: The demand for its products levels off and may even decline. The unemployment resulting from this shift in the structure of demand is also long term.
   (b) Short-term or cyclical unemployment due to unfavorable overall economic conditions. During a recession, demand for automobiles falls off not because of a shift to other producers but because the overall demand for goods has fallen. All producers and workers suffer. This is short-term demand linked to the economic cycle.
3. Poverty results from unemployability due to attributes of the worker that make him or her unsuitable for employment in the production of marketable commodities. Workers who cannot read or otherwise lack appropriate job skills may not be employable regardless of the overall level of demand for labor.

Much unemployment, especially type 2b, can be thought of as the responsibility of the market. It results from the market's failure to accomplish what it is designed to do.

However, some unemployment has less to do with market failure than with individual and social failure (possibly government failure). The market is not designed to provide universal education and basic job skills we associate with the fundamentals of schooling. When workers do not have these skills and, because they are unemployed, cannot afford to acquire them, it is not the market that has failed. The failure is due to society leaving them at the mercy of the market. Correcting the problem can require government intervention.

Liberty and self-determination

Political economy has little to tell us about the poverty of the unemployable except that the solution to their problem will not be found in the market. The market is indifferent to them, and, left to its own devices, will have nothing to do with them.

I have spoken about the assets (including human capacities) that the market values, or finds lacking in value, as though they were things we carry about with us. Economists sometimes speak this way. But it is not always a meaningful and illuminating way to speak about the problem, especially for the unemployable. Those who succeed in making a living through the market sometimes take their ability to do so for granted. But even they may harbor doubts: How competent am I, and how competent am I capable of learning to be? Competent enough? Can I do a job well enough to make my livelihood by selling my abilities (as if they were objects)?

What does it take to make a living? Obviously there is the important matter of job skills or know-how. But beyond the matter of skills, I must have some basic capacities. Am I intelligent enough to understand and capable enough to work within the complex rules, written and unwritten, of the job market: to search for a job, to inquire in appropriate places, to take needed initiative, to interview? Am I capable of learning the complexities of even a simple job: how to add up a check at a restaurant, operate a typewriter or telephone? Can I accept the demand a job makes that I suspend my desire to do something else: to play, to eat, to sleep? Do I understand how to use money, and could I learn given the opportunity? Am I able to take responsibility for myself (e.g., to be at work on time) so that I can devote myself to doing the job I agreed to do to make a living?

However much we take it for granted, our market economy is a complex system; it is a cultural construction of subtlety and intricacy. If we do not master it, we are unemployable. Some of our failings can be corrected by education, but some have to do with our innate capacities and our character. If we do not have the ability to be a part of the culture of the market, we are unemployable and the market can do nothing for us.

What happens to us when the market is our source of livelihood yet we cannot gain a livelihood through the market?

1. We live in poverty without adequate means to provide our subsistence.
2. We depend on family or private charity to meet our basic needs.
3. The government takes responsibility.

As a society, we have opted for the first answer more often than we might care to admit. When the market is indifferent to the plight of the poor, we have followed along echoing that indifference. This is relatively easy to do in a market society, especially if the poor are neither our relatives nor our friends. If they are neither friends nor relatives, then we do not know them or care to know them. We treat their plight as though it has nothing to do with us.

   This indifference is the other side of the disembedded economy discussed in Chapter 1. If the premodern economy was embedded in the larger family unit, then responsibility for welfare resided in the family. We depended for our livelihood on relatives. The disembedded, or "political," economy makes us dependent on strangers who have no obligation to us beyond those implied in the system of property right and contract. This encourages indifference to the plight of others.

   Our attitude of indifference is in some ways imposed on us because there is, in fact, very little we can do individually about the problem of poverty. Capitalism places emphasis on individual opportunity, individual responsibility, and individual achievement. In a capitalist society, we are encouraged to look after ourselves and to look to ourselves. Doing so, it is claimed, will lead to benefits for us and for the nation as a whole.

   Regardless of these benefits, capitalism organizes our economy in a way that impedes concern for the poor. The more we privatize our economic activities, placing the productive means in private hands and subjecting them to private decisions, the less we can do as private citizens to affect the systemic outcomes that make many people poor. When the workings of the market make, or leave, some poor, their poverty does not result from anyone's decision. We do not decide, individually, to create the poor, and we cannot decide individually to do something about poverty. Yet a capitalist economy tends to work against collective decisions regarding economic affairs, and this makes dealing with poverty difficult. Because we can do little individually, and because market society is one centered on individual action and responsibility, the poor will remain so unless government takes responsibility.

   We can put this point another way: In the case of the unemployable, the market is not the appropriate social institution for solving the economic problem of providing the means of life. Market failure is one of the important reasons government must play a role in the economy. More generally, in understanding the role of government, we must know the limits of the market and the appropriate division of labor between market and government. Political economists have debated this issue for over two hundred years. The example of the unemployable suggests one, though not the only, criterion for drawing the line between government and market.

   In drawing this line, we ask: Who is responsible for the fate of the individual in a capitalist economy? How do we think about the distinction between individual and collective responsibility?

   In asking these questions, we encounter a dilemma. A market economy is designed to place responsibility for our lives into our hands. It intends to make us responsible by eliminating, or at least dramatically reducing, the controls and restrictions on actions we can take in pursuit of our interests. It encourages us to act on our own interests rather than those of others or of the community. It also enables us to act on our own interests by expanding the sphere of individual initiative. The more the market economy succeeds in respecting individual rights and validating our pursuit of private ends, the more it places our lives into our own hands. It makes us responsible. Our wealth and poverty, happiness and unhappiness, are of our own making.

The dilemma arises when our liberty acts as an impediment to accomplishing our ends. Liberty can be an impediment to self-determination when (1) the choices we face threaten rather than sustain our autonomy, or (2) the fragility of our capacity for independence demands a structure supporting, rather than simply enabling us to protect, our integrity.

Choices can threaten autonomy when they include options that directly or indirectly weaken independence. Freedom to choose between indigence and a job that demeans us will not sustain our autonomy. Being free to make choices such as this actually undermines our self-respect and sense of ourselves as independent agents in the world.

When we link liberty to self-determination, we assume a well-developed capacity for autonomy that enables the individual to exploit the opportunities available. But this capacity cannot be taken for granted in all cases. Many lack the internal resources needed to take advantage of the opportunities afforded by a society centering on individual choice and responsibility. Indeed, most of us experience this dilemma at one time or another even as adults. When we do so, we need a structure of external support that might help us reconstruct or repair our internal capacities and resources.

Government plays an important part in this process. It provides welfare for those not able to gain remunerative employment at a wage sufficient to maintain what we define as an acceptable standard of living. Government can also supply educational support and services designed to assist individuals in their efforts to gain or regain the capacity for an independent life. For those whose capacities are permanently impaired, government can provide (or finance provision of) the framework for living and support they cannot provide for themselves. Important questions follow: Does our government do an adequate job of providing structure where the person's capacities have been temporarily or permanently impaired? What would be an adequate provision of such a structure, and in which cases is it appropriate for individuals to call on government when they cannot rely on themselves?

The argument suggested here for collective responsibility is, I think, the strongest argument for public education. This argument centers on the link between education and the capacities we need to support our independence. By linking education to freedom (understood as the capacity and opportunity for self-determination), it makes freedom the reason for public education.

Other arguments for collectively providing education also carry weight. Currently, the most popular links education to competitiveness. We must spend more on schooling, provide better schooling, and make students work harder and in a more disciplined way, because that is what (we believe) our competitors are doing or have done.

This sort of argument appeals not to freedom but to the perceived demands of economic progress. Although both arguments may carry weight, and they may even reinforce each other, I think it matters which we employ. The argument based on freedom is clearly much broader in its implications and less contingent in what it demands of us. The argument from competitiveness is contingent in that it makes education a means to economic growth rather than a part of what it means to be an autonomous citizen and full member of society. Because the argument based on freedom directs us to consider the meaning of personhood, it has links to the problem of rights and social justice. It is a rights-based argument, whereas the argument from competitiveness is a welfare-based argument.

Inequality and difference

Differences between us in the way we lead our lives reveal our distinct life choices and express our different characters. Such differences do not bear on questions of virtue and worth. The contemplative life of the scholar or librarian is no more or less virtuous or worthy than the more active life of a lawyer or surgeon. Some of us are more active, some more contemplative, some extroverts, some introverts. Some of us feel more at home in the country, others in the city. If we are fortunate we will find a place in the world that suits our character. What we do, then, has worth for us and may exhibit its own sort of virtue. But it need not place us in relation to others somewhere along a hierarchy of worth or virtue. No moral divide need separate us according to these life choices.

Unlike the differences between persons, inequalities do not reveal life choices and do bear on questions of virtue and worth. Differences are between persons in their capacities as individuals. We assert difference as part of our assertion of our autonomy. Choice plays its part. Inequalities are between persons in their capacities as members of groups. Often these groups are not a matter of choice. That we are men or women, Asian or European, does not express a life choice. When we are treated differently according to involuntary group membership, and when that difference diminishes members of one group, then difference passes over into inequality.

It can be difficult to judge when group membership is voluntary and when it is not. Do Jews and Muslims choose their affiliations? Are heterosexuality and homosexuality matters of preference? Our society tends to divide into groups that experience insiders and outsiders differently. Members of groups celebrate their fellows and disparage others. Again, difference becomes the raw material for inequality. When group membership dominates our self-conceptions and ways of life, the differences between us have more to do with the groups we belong to than with our separate identities and life choices. Inequality is a likely outcome.

As we have seen, markets have less interest in who you are than in what you own. Market society places greater emphasis on individual difference than group identity. And, yet, markets promote vast inequalities based on income and wealth. The group memberships that separated the aristocrat from the peasant give way to those separating income classes: the rich from the poor, the affluent from those who can barely get by.

Because the resulting inequalities depend on amount (of income and wealth), some claim that they express life choices. This would make the inequalities under capitalism a form of difference in the sense I have used the term. It matters, then, why inequalities arise, what part the individual plays in determining his or her place in the hierarchy of income and wealth, and the extent to which inequality of income and wealth means inequality of virtue and worth.

In this chapter we have explored some of the main arguments used to justify inequality. Two lines of thinking guide these arguments. The first dominates the classical argument for inequality, the second the more contemporary arguments that relate income to contribution. The first centers on economic progress, the second on choice.

The classical argument tends to accept class differences and inequality. These differences, however, have an important purpose. They underwrite the process of economic growth and development. Inequality spawns wealth. Without inequality, we remain poor.

Class differences create the means for social saving because the income of one class is the saving of the society as a whole. This income difference, then, leads to capital accumulation, which is the process that takes us from barbarism to civilized society. This is, to use Marx's phrase, the "historical mission of capitalism."

To foster the opportunities wealth affords us, we must be able to produce enough wealth to go around. Doing so requires a prior accumulation of the means for producing the goods and services we need. We must build our producing capacity to a point where it affords some wealth and the opportunities wealth provides to all of us. To do so has meant concentrating wealth into the hands of a class of people devoted to using it for investment rather than consumption.

It was assumed by the classical economists, including Marx, that creating a class of wealthy capitalists and one of impoverished workers is the only way to assure economic progress. The problem, then, was to determine when the process had gone far enough and adequate productive capacity existed for society to give up its preoccupation with investment and growth in favor of other ends. Knowing when we have gone far enough down the road marked out for us by capitalist economic institutions is no easy matter and continues to fuel debate.

The second line of argument for inequality incorporates the premise that inequality of income and wealth can be treated as if it were a difference between persons so long as equal opportunity to become rich is available to all. In this view, inequality is simply one kind of difference, wealthiness the result of a life choice.

This claim raises a set of important questions posed earlier: Can we be equal as persons when we have significantly different amounts of wealth? Is wealth a part of the means for establishing personhood and the measure of success? Why would anyone pursue great wealth if the esteem of others did not follow? If the pursuit of wealth is the pursuit of esteem, then difference in wealth means inequality.

By making livelihood depend on exchange, by concentrating wealth into the hands of an entrepreneurial class, by using wealth as an incentive to save and invest, by attenuating the sense of community obligation in favor of private ends and private property, capitalism creates wealth and poverty. It makes some poor in a way none were poor before: poor because they cannot find work, poor because they have no place in the community, poor because the opportunities for self-determination available to most of their fellows are denied to them. In industrialized societies, today's poor are poor in a world where they need not be and where most are not.

IV

International society

11

International inequality

Interdependence

In the modern world one of the most important groups of which we are members is the nation-state. Our opportunities and life chances are bound up with the nation to which we belong. So also is our sense of who we are: American, Mexican, Chinese, and so on. Because the circumstances of the individual vary in systematic ways with those of the nation, the problems of inequality and difference discussed in Part III for individuals also apply for nations. Important cultural differences distinguish citizens of different nations.[1] These differences form a basis for inequality. We speak of international inequality when we speak of the way our national identity might systematically affect our life chances so that opportunities differ for citizens of different nations. Table 11.1 presents data on some of the important differences between nations that can affect life chances.

International inequality develops in a context of interdependence. Although we differ from citizens of other nations – in culture, in institutions, in affluence, in values – we also depend on citizens of those nations. And our dependence is increasing. The complex mix of difference, inequality, and interdependence presents important and difficult problems. In this chapter and the next, I review some of these problems. I begin with an exploration of international interdependence.

Two senses of economic interdependence between nations have special significance. The first focuses on the division of labor or degree of mutual dependence in production, the second on location of markets. Let me begin with the first.

[1] The idea of a nation differs from that of a state even though the modern state is closely linked to national identity and is sometimes referred to as a "nation-state." The nation is something more and something different from a political unit demarcated by geopolitical boundaries. It is a cultural and historical entity whose boundaries only sometimes conform to those of a politically recognized state.

Table 11.1. *National differences in life chances*

Country	Life expectancy at birth		Persons per physician	Percent of adults literate
	Male	Female		
United States	72	79	404	97
Japan	76	82	609	99
Mexico	68	76	600	88
Iran	64	65	2992	54
Indonesia	59	63	7427	85
Egypt	60	61	616	44
Bangladesh	54	53	6166	35

Source: The World Almanac and Book of Facts: 1993

Economic interdependence in the first sense exists when production in one nation depends on inputs from another. Two nations are economically interdependent when most production processes in one require a single vital input from the other. Thus Japan's economy may be considered interdependent with that of the oil-producing nations of the Middle East even if Japan requires only one input (oil) from those nations. It happens that this one input is used in the production of most goods produced in Japan and thus is vital to the entire Japanese economy.

Interdependence in production also exists when the goods produced and consumed in each country employ a set of inputs from the other. Interdependence in this sense suggests that although the two nations are politically separate, in important respects they share one economy.

Rather than defining interdependence as mutual dependence in production, we can define it in terms of markets and demand. This is the second sense of interdependent. If a country, such as Japan, sells a significant proportion of its output to another country, say, the United States, then the level of economic activity in Japan will depend on the level of demand for goods in the United States. A recession in the United States will depress demand for imports from Japan. Indeed, on the assumption that the proportion of income spent on imports is more or less fixed, imports will fall in proportion to the fall in the level of economic activity in the United States.

The nature and degree of interdependence between countries vary over time and from country to country. Up to a point, they also vary with national economic policies – whether governments encourage free trade or restrict imports. Restrictive policies can reduce interdependence. It is generally thought that the degree of economic interdependence has increased notably during the post–World War II period (see Cooper 1972). This has been especially important in the United States, where the implications of interdependence are now being felt in ways that are novel and disturbing.

Interdependence may be more or less symmetrical. That is, one country may be dependent on another, while the other is more or less autonomous. The Japanese are dependent on markets in the United States to a degree far exceeding the dependence of U.S. corporations on sales in Japan. Many less developed countries are dependent on oil imports from petroleum-exporting countries, while the latter are not similarly dependent on those less developed countries for necessary inputs.

Asymmetries in interdependence are important both economically and politically. Economically, they make one country or group of countries sensitive to economic policies and economic cycles in other countries not so dependent themselves. Politically, asymmetries create power relations between countries and vulnerabilities open to political exploitation. They give those less dependent leverage over those more dependent (see Keohane and Nye 1977).

If, by accident or policy, a country remains self-sufficient, we speak of its economy as *autarchic*. Economic autarchy refers to the absence of interdependence. Domestic production processes are not significantly dependent on inputs from abroad, and the level of domestic economic activity is not significantly affected by the state of markets abroad.

Autarchy has advantages and disadvantages paralleling those of interdependence. The main advantage of autarchy is domestic control over the nation's economic destiny. Interdependence seriously limits the nation's ability to chart its own course. Rather, its fate is determined by the world economy or by powerful nations and international organizations (such as the International Monetary Fund). The main disadvantage of autarchy is that it excludes the nation from the benefits of trade, of markets in which to sell its produce and of access to goods produced in other countries. Let me consider the advantages and disadvantages of interdependence more closely, beginning with the advantages.

The advantages of interdependence arise from expansion of markets and market opportunities. Expansion of markets offers potential gains (1) in productivity, (2) in income and employment, and (3) in welfare stemming from access to lower cost consumer goods.

Increasing productivity means higher levels of production (assuming employment does not shrink), and this demands growth in markets to absorb the higher levels of output. In one of his most famous formulations, Adam Smith tells us that "the division of labor is limited by the extent of the market."

We can put the same idea in more general language. Adam Smith's vision ties economic growth to what economists refer to as increasing returns to scale. Increasing returns to scale means that as the amount produced increases, unit costs fall. Thus, for example, it is much cheaper per car for General Motors to produce 400,000 cars annually than to produce only 100. One of the reasons for this is that larger scale production affords opportunities for extending the division of labor. But there are other reasons as well. One of the most important has to do with plant and equipment. When purchase of the most advanced technology requires a large investment in plant and equipment, this will only be feasible if production can be maintained on a comparably large scale. To utilize the investment profitably, the market must be large enough to absorb output in quantities much greater than those needed for smaller investments. The extent of the market helps define the kind of capital stock it will prove profitable to acquire, and thus the unit costs of production. When the more costly capital stock has a greater productive capacity and yields lower unit costs, the extent of the market becomes a major determinant of labor productivity.

Finding new markets facilitates productivity growth. Because economic interdependence means access to new markets (in other countries), it provides opportunities for market expansion. If the size of the home market impedes growth in productivity, access to international trade can enable domestic producers to reap the benefits of economies of scale. If lower production costs lead to lower prices, benefits of a widening market attendant on expanded participation in the world economy will accrue to consumers as cheaper domestic goods.

In addition to productivity gains, interdependence can lead to gains in output and employment. For an economy operating at less than full capacity, the opportunity to sell abroad is an opportunity to expand domestic levels of production and employment. Doing so increases domestic incomes and thus domestic consumption.

As we have seen, in capitalist economies, income depends on employment and employment on the demand for labor. Labor is hired to produce goods; thus the demand for labor depends on the demand for goods. Because the demand for goods varies with incomes, a circular relationship develops among income, demand, and employment. Because of the circularity of the economic flow, an addition to demand stimulates a sequence of further additions. In other words, it multiplies.

Foreign demand stimulates domestic production, which stimulates employment and income. The additional domestic incomes created by production for foreign markets stimulate further additions to home production – thus additional income, employment, and demand. The eventual effect of the export market on domestic income and employment is a multiple of the magnitude of exports. The size of the multiplier varies with the rate of domestic saving and the proportion of domestic income spent on imports.

The foregoing holds even if we ignore the possible impact of exports on investment. But export markets can also stimulate new investment in plant and equipment. This new investment will stimulate demand and employment. The circularity of the economic process assures that the impact of the initial investment stimulus also multiplies in its effect on incomes and employment.

Thus, if domestic markets are inadequate to maintain full utilization of domestic capital and labor, exploitation of world markets can fill the gap. Greater economic interdependence can enhance the domestic level of economic activity (see Robinson 1966). Countries that succeed in capturing world markets for their domestic products employ workers and generate incomes in selling to consumers and producers abroad. Such countries garner to (some of) their citizens a share of the wealth of other nations, turning that wealth into their incomes.

Matters appear differently for the country at the receiving end of the exports. When imports meet a need that can be and has been met in the past by domestic producers, they displace domestic products. The income formerly used to buy a domestically produced good is now spent on a good produced abroad. Rather than enhancing the levels of economic activity and employment domestically, it enhances those levels abroad. If this happens, trade moves income, wealth, and employment from one country to another, and the gain for one is at the expense of, and in proportion to the loss of, another.

A third gain from interdependence accrues to buyers of imported goods. Producers can gain from access to cheaper inputs available from abroad, whereas consumers gain from access to cheaper consumer goods produced abroad. In the classical theory, this advantage stems from productivity differences across countries (or regions). Each country supplies others with goods it is relatively more efficient in producing. All benefit.

If we take productivity differences between nations to be given, we can imagine a global division of labor that takes advantage of those differences. Global specialization allows buyers to acquire goods from those best situated to produce them. This conclusion focuses our attention on efficient use of labor and other resources. It does not take into account the impact of trade on the level of output and employment as that reflects the global distribution of market shares. Further on, I explore this issue in greater detail.

Each of these advantages of interdependence carries risks: (1) Just as exports expand our markets, imports reduce them; (2) the opportunity to sell abroad may or may not mean expansion of domestic production; and (3) interdependence weakens autonomy and the possibility of domestic economic self-determination.

If greater interdependence means a higher propensity to import, then, given the rate of investment, it means a lower level of economic activity. The impact of investment on domestic demand is dampened by the leakage of demand into purchases of foreign goods. Similarly, government budget deficits expand domestic income, but by a smaller amount because a larger part of income is spent on goods produced abroad. An open economy can be a larger economy or it can be a smaller economy, depending on the competitiveness of domestically produced goods.

The question of competitiveness carries particular weight for latecomers to modern industrial technology. Because costs tend to fall as the scale of production increases, those producers who, because of a longer history in a particular market, have larger markets also have a competitive advantage. If producers in countries at early stages of industrial development are disadvantaged, they may benefit from government protection aimed at giving them the opportunity to catch up both in technology and in scale of production.[2]

Even if goods produced by domestic firms are competitive and openness expands markets, those producers may not expand their domestic capital investments to meet growing markets. They can meet growing markets by investing abroad. If they do so, the income and employment benefits of trade accrue to other countries. The question who gains from interdependence, then, is not simply a question about the competitiveness of goods produced by domestic firms but about where those firms choose to produce those goods.

General Motors can produce for the U.S. market in the United States or Mexico. If it produces more cheaply in Mexico, G.M. benefits, but the U.S. economy does not, and indeed may suffer loss of employment and income. Critics of the North American Free Trade Agreement have emphasized these dangers of interdependence (see Koechlin and Larudee 1992).

The fact that U.S. firms make decisions concerning where to produce based not on the benefits or harms to the U.S. economy but on the likely impact of the decision on the firm's profitability should caution us against identifying the corporate interest with the national interest. What is good for

---

[2] Those schooled in the theory of comparative advantage tend to dismiss arguments centering on competitiveness because such arguments emphasize absolute rather than relative advantages in productivity. See, for example, Krugman and Obstfeld (1992, Chapter 2). But competitive advantages can be important so long as productivity differences depend on market scale, and therefore market share, and so long as we do not assume a tendency toward full employment. I explore the notion of comparative advantage at greater length later.

G.M. may not be good for America. The health of "our" corporations bears a complex relation to the health of "our" economy. If national economic policy targets the domestic economy, it may conflict with the interests of firms legally domiciled within the nation's borders or historically identified with domestic economic activities.

Finally, openness to world trade reduces domestic control over the economy. When employment at home depends on exports, employment is made vulnerable to the effects of recession abroad. And when we import goods, we can find that we also import inflation along with those goods. Not only are we affected by economic affairs outside our borders and thus less under our control, but our government's capacity to guide our economy diminishes.

In a closed economy, when government spending stimulates economic activity, it affects domestic income and employment. In an open economy, part of the impact drains off in purchases abroad. If we spend a portion of our income on imports, increasing incomes increases imports. Because stimulating incomes does not stimulate exports, doing so adversely affects the balance of trade (the difference between exports and imports). Thus, in an open economy, government economic policy encounters a difficulty not present in a closed economy. The impact of policy on domestic employment is less because incomes are used to buy goods produced abroad.

If we value our ability to control our economic destiny, openness of our economy can be harmful. This harm is felt in limitations of government control. It is also felt in the vulnerability attendant upon interdependence. If we require oil imports to sustain domestic production of goods and services, then our destiny depends on decisions made by oil exporters and circumstances in oil-producing regions. The same holds true for dependence on markets abroad. In an export-oriented economy, domestic income and employment (therefore welfare) are inextricably linked with the world market. This makes the nation vulnerable, especially to those foreign countries whose nationals purchase a large part of the goods exported.

The more widespread our interdependence, the greater our vulnerability to events in other parts of the world. Economic interdependence poses political challenges because we are dependent on forces we may not control. We no longer rule our own destiny.

Growing economic interdependence carries with it a challenge to national sovereignty so far as sovereignty is tied up with national self-determination. National self-determination, on a political level, involves such matters as the security of national borders and the autonomy of domestic political decision making. Political sovereignty is weak in nations vulnerable to invasion or susceptible to political subversion domestically by forces supported from outside.

But political sovereignty means more than the security of borders an˒

protection against the subversion of domestic political process. It also means a capacity for the nation to determine its direction: to pursue economic development as a national goal, to pursue welfare state economic policies should it choose to do so, to define its own economic institutions (e.g., that lean more or less in the direction of free markets). Economic interdependence can reduce the ability of government to accomplish these goals. It can place their accomplishment into the hands of the impersonal forces of the global market and the not so impersonal forces of other national interests.

The North American Free Trade Agreement has encountered opposition for reasons connected to these problems (see Friedman 1992). Under a free trade regime, U.S. firms can evade environmental or occupational health and safety regulations by moving production south of the border. If this happens, we purchase job safety and clean environment at the expense of income and employment. If this is likely, interdependence and openness can erode sovereignty and with it the nation's capacity to define itself and pursue its own ends.

Trade and the global division of labor

The classical economists analyzed international relations assuming that nations were interdependent, but only to a limited degree. David Ricardo developed one of the most influential arguments for free trade assuming limited interdependence (1951, Chapter VII). He argued that free trade would lead to a global division of labor allocating production of different goods to those nations capable of producing them relatively more efficiently. His theory is termed the theory of comparative advantage.

The theory sets out from a distinction between *absolute* and *comparative* advantage. A nation has an absolute advantage over another nation in the production of a good when it can produce that good using fewer inputs per unit of output. The classical economists focused on labor cost, so absolute advantage meant lower unit labor requirements (or higher labor productivity). By contrast, comparative advantage referred to differences between nations in the relation between labor productivity in the production of different goods. A country has a comparative advantage, say, in the production of cheese, when the ratio between its labor productivities in cheese and wine exceeds that ratio in another country. The country specializing in cheese is proportionally rather than absolutely more productive in that good.[3]

---

[3] Under autarchy, the domestic exchange rate of cheese for wine depends on the relation between their costs. If we are mainly concerned with labor costs, as the classics were, and take wage rates to be uniform, then the exchange rate depends on unit labor requirements. We benefit from trade if we can purchase more wine for our cheese abroad than we can at

The theory of comparative advantage suggests that these two countries can engage in mutually beneficial trade, with the first specializing in cheese and the second in wine. It also suggests that such mutual benefits exist even if the second country has an absolute advantage in both cheese and wine. Each country would specialize in production of those goods in which it had a relative advantage in productivity.

The theory of comparative advantage is a *theory* about the benefits of trade and specialization. It is important to bear this in mind because the term comparative advantage is sometimes used not to refer to a theory of global specialization and trade but simply to describe situations where nations specialize and trade different goods. The existence of specialization does not imply the workings of the forces summarized in the theory of comparative advantage. The latter carries a set of special assumptions, such as full employment of labor and other resources and that relative productivities are given independently of trade, that may or may not hold. It explains trade in a special way that may or may not be illuminating for particular cases, even those in which nations specialize in ways the theory might predict.

The theory of comparative advantage focuses our attention on differences in productivity within and across nations. Ricardo did not much specify what factors were responsible for differences in labor productivity in different countries (thus what accounts for the greater efficiency of certain global distributions of production over others). It makes a difference whether we emphasize the level of technical know-how and capital investment or the natural fertility of the earth. The former is a product of history and shaped by social institutions, possibly influenced by economic and social policies. The latter is often assumed to be given, a force that shapes but is not shaped by the historical process (see Blecker 1992a).[4]

In the classical comparative advantage conception, different countries produce different goods, each specializing in what it does best. If the world economy conformed to this image, imports would not displace domestic

---

home. Whether we can depends on the exchange rate of cheese for wine abroad. We stand to benefit from trade when the amount of wine we can purchase with a unit of cheese is less at home than abroad or, equivalently, the wine price of cheese is less at home. But this will be the case when the ratio of unit labor requirements between cheese and wine is lower at home than abroad, thus when home has a comparative advantage in cheese. Under these conditions, we are better off using our labor to produce cheese and using our cheese to buy wine abroad than by dividing home labor between cheese and wine. Formally, let y represent labor productivity, c and w cheese and wine respectively, and $*$ the other or foreign country. Then the condition summarized in this paragraph for comparative advantage is

$$\frac{y_c}{y_w} + \frac{y_c^*}{y_w^*}$$

[4] This may not be entirely accurate because what we recognize as a "resource" and the amount available of it vary with history and technology.

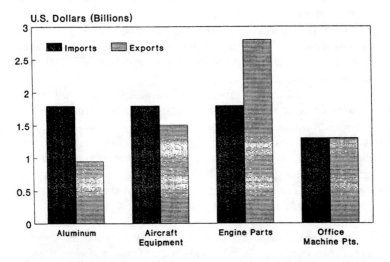

Figure 11.1. Intraindustry trade between the United States and Canada, 1990.
Source: United States Free Trade Highlights, 1990.

products but would enhance the welfare of domestic consumers. Domestic incomes would vary with the qualities of domestic resources. Countries would not fare better because their producers were more competitive and thus able to displace producers elsewhere.

In this vision, the world economy is a harmonious place. Gains in welfare for one country are not at the expense of another. Rather, they reflect the accidents of endowments in different countries.

The implied argument for free trade runs into difficulty when the trading partners compete over markets for the same goods rather than specializing in the different products in which each has its relative advantage. When nations sell the same sorts of goods to each other, they are said to engage in *intra*industry trade (see Figure 11.1 for examples from United States–Canada trade). Such trade challenges the image of the global economy fostered by the theory of comparative advantage.[5]

Specialization may follow competition over market shares when the less competitive are driven from the market. The less the pattern of trade follows that of resource endowment, the less it implies an efficient use of geographically distributed resources. From the standpoint of the geographic distribu-

---

[5] Note that product differentiation means that goods sold are similar, serving in a broad sense the same purpose, but not necessarily the same. Personal computers produced in the United States and abroad are broadly the same goods, but will not exhibit all the same features.

tion of resource endowments, the pattern of trade seems more and more arbitrary.[6]

This does not make free trade a bad idea; but it does make the virtues of free trade problematic. We need, then, to look more closely at the circumstances in different nations to evaluate the benefits and harms of openness to trade.

Clearly, the vision of world production organized by prior location of inputs clearly fits poorly when the primary inputs are not location specific. We can speak of certain countries having an advantage in production of certain goods when it matters where those goods are produced. It matters for many primary products: oranges, bananas, coffee. It also matters for minerals such as gold and cobalt. But why should it matter where you produce cars, computers, or shirts? For the latter, the capital investment can be located wherever an appropriate labor supply, transportation system, and perhaps political environment exist. And it is the location of the capital investment that determines who gets the employment and associated incomes. In such cases, the problem of the location of investment, with its profound implications for national economic life, cannot be resolved by asking where resource endowments make it (relatively) more efficient to produce. The increasing importance of trade in manufactured goods rather than primary products significantly alters the terms of the classical debate over free trade.

Wealth and poverty

Why are some nations rich and others poor? The answer to this question involves historical processes of long duration and considerable complexity. The fortunes of particular countries depend on factors ranging from the way citizens are, or are not, educated to the way the nation organizes its banking system. More generally, however, we can identify the crucial forces operating and how their effects are differently experienced in different countries.

The nature and causes of global inequality are not historically fixed. The basic forces change over time; and our explanation of inequality must change with them. As a brief introduction to the problem, I will work with a simple scheme that distinguishes two types of global political economy and therefore two types of international inequality. This scheme distinguishes between two circumstances: (1) an interdependent world economy based on specialization in production, and (2) a world economy in which competition over markets plays the primary organizing role. Of course we generally face a

---

[6] One observer suggests the geographic distribution of production might be arbitrary in important respects; see Krugman (1991).

mix of the two. Still, the balance of the mix has importance, as I will try to indicate. I begin with the first type, and in the next section consider the second.

The image of a global economy of the first type is in many ways the classical image of the founders of political economy. It remains influential, although its relevance has diminished, especially in the post–World War II period. Thinking in this image, we treat the world economy as a global division of labor. By the term global division of labor, I have in mind a system of economic interdependence in which different countries produce different goods and in which exchange circulates goods to countries that need them but do not produce them. This image of a global division of labor mirrors that of a domestic division of labor as depicted by Adam Smith in the *Wealth of Nations*.

Inequalities that arise within a global division of labor must have something to do with differences in what countries specialize in. These differences relate to the varying capacities of countries to produce and sell different goods. Differences in capacities are crucial. We need to explore not only their implications but also how they arise in the first place. A question of special importance is the following: Do differences in capacities result from built-in differences in regional or national endowments, or are they the result of historical processes? Are they fixed, or can they be altered as the development process unfolds?

The emergence of inequalities suggests that it might matter what a nation produces; some specialties might lead to more rapid growth in wealth than others. What about specialization could lead to differentials in the growth of wealth? What determines how nations and regions specialize? The answers to these questions have much to do with the relation among wages, incomes, productivity, and the growth of the market (see Lewis 1978).

Recall that the wage is both a cost of production and a primary component of the market for the goods produced. The higher the wage, and thus the income of the worker in a given region, the greater the cost of production there. But, at the same time, the higher the wage and income of the worker, the larger the market. Workers in countries with higher wages have higher incomes and form the foundation for a wider home market for domestically produced goods. On the other side, low wage levels inhibit the growth of the home market. To understand the development of international specialization and inequality, we need to pay special attention to this two-sided quality of the relation of wages to capitalist development.

Adam Smith's theorem relating the division of labor to the extent of the market has relevance here. The extent of the market depends in part on the level of incomes. Higher incomes mean more purchasing power, which implies greater scope for development of the domestic division of labor.

Large and growing markets encourage domestic investment, accumulation of capital, and the growth of national wealth.

Countries with relatively expensive labor and an institutional structure conducive to investment in plant and equipment gained ground on other countries with cheaper labor and institutional impediments to investment. Some of these impediments originated in restrictions that colonial powers placed on their colonies, restrictions concerning what could and could not be produced. The world order that emerged resulted from both economic and political forces operating to determine a global division of labor favoring some countries and limiting opportunities for development in others. A process of unequal development ensued between the two groups of countries.

This process led to the division of the global economy into the industrially developed "north" and the un- (or under) developed "south." The uneven development of the global economy divided it into economic regions. The uneven development of nations then follows that of regions, with nations encompassing more or less successful regions. Two not entirely hypothetical examples may clarify that process.

Example 1: Assume, first, that your country has resources specially suited to produce cotton. The soil and climate make labor devoted to raising cotton unusually productive. To produce cotton, you need a relatively small investment of capital goods and the funds to support unskilled agricultural (slave) labor. These costs are not great because the labor is unskilled and the worker has traditionally survived on little and has low expectations. Your labor costs are low and the productivity of your labor in the production of cotton is relatively high not because of division of labor or the presence of advanced equipment but because the land is especially fertile for cotton growing.

Your workers produce much of their own subsistence. Their productivity in this noncommercial subsistence agricultural sector is low, as is their standard of living. Your labor force produces enough subsistence goods to feed themselves and a cotton crop available for commercial sale in exchange for luxury goods consumed by the plantation owners and a margin for expansion of investment in plantation production (e.g., acquisition of more slaves).

You export cotton, but only generate enough subsistence to reproduce the agricultural workers who produce the cotton. You do not produce an excess, or surplus, of subsistence goods to support an urban work force in manufacturing. Your surplus is cotton. You are very productive and thus highly competitive in cotton production, but you are relatively unproductive in agricultural subsistence goods. As a result, your workers have a low standard of living, acquire most of it by producing it themselves, and cannot support workers in other sectors with the export of any excess subsistence goods. These characteristics limit the size of your domestic market and prevent diversification of your work force into pursuits that take them away from agriculture, where they can contribute to production of their subsistence.

You sell your cotton abroad rather than at home. It will be used elsewhere to produce manufactured goods, some of which you may even import for your own use. You are able to specialize in cotton production because productivity is high and costs are low.

The workers who produce your cotton have little income and can afford to buy little. In producing cotton you need invest in little machinery, mainly the cost of slaves and land, if acquiring land costs you anything.

This seems advantageous from the capitalist's point of view. Yet these advantages for the individual capitalist do not play out well for the nation as a whole. Low levels of investment mean little stimulus to aggregate demand and therefore little growth of the home market. Low levels of workers' income do little to stimulate a manufacturing sector. The economy stagnates even if the cotton sector thrives.

From the point of view of Adam Smith's concern, the growth of a wealthy nation, specializing in cotton manufacture is not at all a good idea. Yet, from the point of view of the calculation made by the profit-seeking capitalist of Adam Smith's own vision, specialization in cotton production is a very good idea. When deciding how to specialize within the global division of labor, the decision will favor specializing in cotton because the productivity of labor is high in cotton production and the kind of labor available is suitable. The combination of low wages, low capital investment, and high productivity of land in cotton production makes a few plantation owners rich and keeps the nation poor.

Example 2: Now, assume your country is not particularly suited to cotton production. Your land is not particularly fertile, and labor is relatively expensive. The labor is more expensive for two interconnected reasons. First, the workers' way of life is different. They are treated more as full citizens, with attendant rights and responsibilities. This treatment brings with it an expectation that their level of living will meet a higher standard, one appropriate to free men and women and property owners, even if their property is only their labor. Second, productivity in agriculture has reached a higher level due in part to a long historical development. More productive labor generates more means of consumption per person and higher living standards. The greater productivity of labor in agriculture plays a particularly important role in supporting a higher living standard.

Those domestic capitalists not settled in the more fertile, lower wage, southern climates seek their fortunes in the north. They do not have the resources to set themselves up in plantation agriculture, which would not be viable anyway. But they have some know-how in manufacturing and some limited access to capital to invest in plant and equipment. They set themselves up as domestic manufacturers.

These domestic capitalists hire workers whom they must pay higher wages than their southern counterparts. That is, they can pay higher wages due to the greater productivity of agriculture, and they must do so because of the level of living expected by their workers. Domestic investment is high due to the aggregate of all their efforts, and domestic wages are strong whether they like it or not. Thus the domestic market is also strong and growing. The wealth of the nation is expanding. Adam Smith is at home, and all is right with the world.

As the manufacturers expand their investments to keep up with growing demand, their unit costs fall, as Smith would have predicted. The division of labor develops with the growth of the market, and labor productivity improves both because of the larger size of establishments and the invention of ever more productive technology. The process of creative destruction sets in. This process is made possible by the growth of the home market. The lack of a growing home market bars the southern nations from benefiting.

The global division of labor favors manufacturing countries at the expense of agricultural. Manufacturing fosters technical improvements that can raise the productivity of labor in agriculture, which is a necessary condition for economic development. Manufacturing favors urbanization, which expands the market-dependent part of the population and therefore, at least potentially, the scale of the home market. Manufacturing encourages technical change and product development, thereby expanding opportunities for market development and new investment. Manufacturing and urbanization stimulate attitudes conducive to encouraging capitalist enterprise, attitudes favorable to the pursuit of private gain, innovation, and capital investment.

The higher wages in the north stimulate the growth of the domestic market, which stagnates in the south. The world economy becomes a world of rich and poor nations where international inequality stems from differences in wages and in the organization of production. It has much to do with the great divide between manufacturing and agriculture, urban and rural. Profit seeking and private accumulation benefit some countries but not others.

The global division of markets

Economic development has meant evolution away from a world dominated by a global division of labor. With development, costs of transportation decline, reducing or eliminating the advantage of producing in close proximity to markets. Increasing size and scale of production, together with an emerging global perspective, reduce the firm's orientation toward production in its home country. Adam Smith and David Ricardo both believed that producers would naturally invest their profits at home, in part for patriotic reasons, in part because they felt more secure doing so. But in the world of commerce, patriotism is no match for the calculation of cost and profitability. Producers produce where it is most profitable to do so.

Natural advantage plays less of a role in the geographic location of manufacturing. Because of this, geographic considerations per se do not explain the location of industry. This means, in brief, that firms, whatever their country of origin, strive to produce where production is least costly and sell where they can find the best markets.

As economic development enhances the weight of manufactured goods in trade, the image of a global division of labor recedes. Instead of exporting and importing different kinds of goods, we export and import groups of goods that are broadly similar. We can still wonder whether doing so brings prosperity. The answer follows closely the vicissitudes of domestic producers in a world of international competition.

The benefits and harms of participation in the global economy come to depend primarily on factors affecting the competitive position of domestic producers. We can judge competitive position by the trend over time in global market shares for relevant industries. Contraction (expansion) of market shares suggests declining (increasing) competitiveness.[7] A strong competitive position in world markets brings with it higher levels of domestic output and investment. What kinds of factors determine our competitive position in the world economy?

Economists continue to debate this question. The factors claimed to explain failure range broadly: Labor costs are too high, the work force is poorly educated, capital stock is outdated, corporate strategies are too shortsighted, government is too heavily involved in the economy, government is not involved enough, and so on.

Many of these theories (though probably not all) have merit. I will not attempt to sort them here. We can, however, discern a common theme running through many of the theories. The competitive position of domestic industry in the world economy depends on the quality of productive inputs as compared with those available to competitors. Quality of productive inputs has a number of dimensions: cost, productivity, reliability, skill, to name a few. We will do better if we have newer and better equipment, equally or better skilled but less costly labor, and more competent management.

---

[7] For a fuller discussion of competitiveness and trade, see Blecker (1992b).

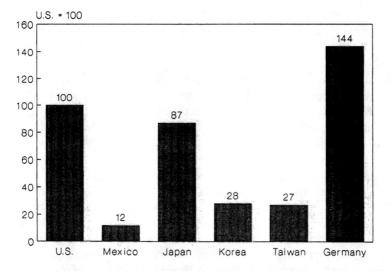

Figure 11.2. Hourly compensation index, international comparisons, 1990. *Source:*
Monthly Labor Review (Capdevielle 1991).

Because where firms sell does not determine where they produce, the
home market becomes less important than their ability to exploit a global
market. Because of this, the firms' interest can diverge from that of the
nation. It becomes vital, then, for the nation to make its economic policies
independent, to a significant degree, of corporate interests.

The link between wages and the scale of the market historically implied
that high wages, by stimulating the home market, encourage capital accumulation. In modern economies, high wages attract sellers but not producers. High wages no longer encourage capital investment. This does not
bode well for those nations (such as the United States) that benefited from
rising living standards during that period when the home market played a
decisive role in economic development.

If labor productivity in relevant U.S. industries is not significantly higher
than in Hong Kong, South Korea, or Mexico, for example, and wages there
are significantly lower than in the United States, producers located in the
United States will have difficulty competing. Figure 11.2 presents a sample
of data of hourly compensation costs in different countries.[8] The figure
suggests that the U.S. competitive position vis-à-vis Mexico, Korea, and
Hong Kong is not strong for industries in which labor costs play a significant

---

[8] Hourly compensation costs include direct pay (e.g., wages) and other employee expenditures
for insurance, benefit programs, and labor taxes.

role and transportation costs do not. It also suggests that labor costs will not explain our competitive failure vis-à-vis other competitors, such as Japan, where costs are close to ours, and Germany, where they are substantially greater.[9]

Obviously, higher productivity abroad compounds the problem. Wages in South Korea challenge living standards in the United States when producers in South Korea increase their market shares at the expense of U.S. producers. Our competitive position in the world economy deteriorates. To maintain living standards in the United States, or any higher wage economy, means accomplishing one or more of the following goals:

1. Increase productivity relative to competitors. This requires high levels of investment in new capital stock embodying more productive technology, high levels of expenditure on research and development, higher quality labor, and improved organization and management of industry. Of course, even if you succeed in raising levels of investment and R&D expenditures, this may or may not improve productivity relative to your competitors, who are already investing at a higher rate than you are. High rates of investment tend to follow high rates of market expansion. It is difficult to build new capital when the old is underutilized. Nonetheless, government policies aimed at encouraging investment in plant and equipment and research expenditures speak directly to the problem of competitive failure.

2. Specialize in production of goods for which wage differentials do not matter. The lower the proportion of costs made up of wages (the higher made up of capital and materials) the less disadvantageous are higher wages in the competitive struggle.[10]

3. Protect domestic producers from foreign competition by erecting barriers to imports.

4. Accept the decline of competitiveness and stagnation of incomes, focusing attention on ameliorating effects rather than attacking causes. This entails redistributing a given (or slowly growing) output to protect living standards of those affected by loss of markets: expand the government sector; redistribute income to provide income supports and more fairly apportion the burden of waning competitiveness; focus on a socially acceptable living standard rather than continual improvement in real incomes.

Politically, the third solution often gains ground during hard times. It takes us back to Adam Smith's argument with the mercantilists, and deserves closer consideration. It raises, once again, the great question of the benefits and dangers of trade.

---

[9] Exchange rate changes have significant impact on comparisons for the advanced industrial societies.

[10] This strategy refers us back to product life-cycle arguments concerning the global distribution of productive activities; see Vernon (1966).

If our competitive position is strong, then we might oppose restraints on trade because they can only impede the growth of our markets and the expansion of domestic income and employment.[11] If our competitive position is weak, domestic interests favor restraints on imports. They hope that forcing consumers to buy domestically produced goods will secure markets for home industry. Doing so, it is hoped, will also secure incomes and employment.

Posed in this way, the problem of restraint on trade looms as a political one that pits the nation as consumer against the nation as producer. As producer and worker we favor restraints, but as consumers we favor open markets so that we can buy what we want (sometimes imported goods) at the best price we can get. Of course, consumers must also work, and their interests depend on the vulnerability of their work to competition from producers abroad.

If a struggle between interest groups determines our trade policy, we should have little reason to expect that policy to benefit the nation as a whole or serve the national interest. On the contrary, such policy will likely serve the interests of the more powerful groups. Those interests may be in trade restrictions that protect poorly organized and poorly run industry at the expense of the consumer. The national interest in economic growth and development will only by accident be served by policies put in place at the behest of those influential with government officials and elected representatives.

Although those who study politics often emphasize this dimension of the problem, questions remain concerning how policy might be tailored to serve the broader interest of the nation in the welfare of the people. Ideology looms large here because it often plays a crucial role in defining the national interest (see Krasner 1978). In the United States, government typically adheres to the doctrine of free trade accepting the classical argument that all will benefit from open markets. This belief encourages free trade policies, yet often runs up against vested domestic interests that expect to lose out if not protected from foreign competition. Trade policy, then, follows not only a struggle between domestic interest groups but also a struggle between interests and ideology.

If we attempt to stand above private interest, we need to know the national interest in the area of trade, and the policy most likely to advance that interest. For economists, such a policy is one that would revive competitiveness and thus strengthen the national economy.

---

[11] We might not. Why give up advantages unless you are compelled to do so? If a country can maintain domestic monopolies or near monopolies for their own producers and yet sell extensively abroad, little in the way of economic argument stands in their way.

I cannot say if such a policy exists. Those favoring free trade consider it hard medicine, but the medicine most likely to make domestic producers more productive and efficient, inasmuch as they will have to be more efficient to survive. Restraints on trade allow domestic producers to remain inefficient by international standards. Advocates of free trade consider restraints an encouragement to slovenliness. By limiting competition, they reduce the pressure to produce efficiently, improve productivity, and enhance product quality. Even if this is true, however, it does not follow that free trade will assure that domestic producers will become more efficient and competitive. They might just go out of business.

It is always important to bear in mind that a capitalist world economy is a competitive world economy. It is a world of winners and losers. Domestic growth depends on the exploitation of international markets. If each nation could develop within a particular sector, and trade its output to other nations that have specialized differently, the world economy would be one of mutual or reciprocal advantage. This is, once again, the world economy of a global division of labor. It has its own risks because, as we have seen, it matters how countries specialize.

But in the modern world economy, competitive success for a country does not mean success in marketing a single product or a limited group of products. It may start out that way (e.g., with cheap textiles), but the characteristics of the domestic economy that made its firms so competitive in a restricted area are soon found to apply more broadly. Those high-quality inputs can be used to produce any (manufactured) good more efficiently than the competition. Because of this, the more competitive countries or regions produce for and sell to the world. They become wealthy by appropriating the markets in other countries. International competition brings with it a concentration rather than a dispersion of production and investment. It implies that economic development will be an uneven process, favoring some and injuring others.

Instead of being advantageous to all, international competition is advantageous to those regions and nations whose industries are the most competitive. Those nations produce for and sell to the world. They not only produce their own wealth, but their success in international competition means that their markets are wider and expand more rapidly than do those of their less successful competitors. The rapid expansion of their markets means rapid accumulation at home and rapid growth in domestic incomes. But it also means a narrowing and slower growth of markets for their competitors. The world economy grows unequally; global growth concentrates rather than diffusing.

This observation suggests a dilemma for those countries (such as the

United States) whose competitive position is waning. Protection of industry through trade restrictions can sustain rather than cure the disease. It allows us to live with our failings rather than do something about them. Protecting the domestic market secures demand but may throw an obstacle in the path of growth.

Whether protection impedes growth depends on the size of the domestic market and the likely dynamism of industry in a protected environment. Closing off a large domestic market for domestic producers enables them to enjoy the benefits of economies of scale. These benefits might be lost in an open economy because the growth of domestic producers will be limited, and even curtailed, by competition from more efficient foreign producers. By keeping foreign competition out, the gains in productivity that come from exploiting a large domestic market accrue to domestic producers. These domestic producers may, in time, become sufficiently productive to compete successfully in the world market.

Protection makes this possible but provides no guarantee. For the trick to work, domestic producers must use the home market as the basis for new capital investment embodying more efficient production methods. They must face strong incentives to modernize and produce efficiently even though they are protected from foreign competition. Domestic competition might play an important role here, which brings us back to the problem of the size of the domestic market. A large home market can sustain a number of competing producers in an industry keeping that industry competitive even when protected from foreign competition. In a small market this might prove difficult. Thus a smaller country may need to protect its home market without losing access to the world market if it is to become competitive. It needs to combine import restrictions with an export oriented growth strategy.

The policy of free trade subjects the economy to the vicissitudes of international competition and the unequal growth implied in the competitive process. No international law assures success to participants. Only some can succeed because their success comes at the expense of their competitors. Contrary to what we are sometimes told, we have no special claim to be number one (see Gordon 1986). If we compete, we are at least as likely to come in tenth as first, to lose markets to other nations as to win over theirs.

This is the dilemma faced by countries whose competitive position is weak. Withdrawal from the world economy protects domestic producers and the incomes they generate. But, by limiting access to global markets, protection of the home market protects domestic producers at a cost: the potential gains in productivity available to producers in rapidly growing markets. Participation in the world economy provides no assurance that we will become more efficient, and can mean a continuing loss of markets, incomes, and employment. The dilemma is made worse by the fact that in a capitalist economy, growth is necessary to maintain demand and employment. Where growth fails, we do not simply maintain a steady course at a fixed level, we lose ground.

As we have seen, political economy sometimes employs the concept of a global division of labor to characterize the organization of the world economy. This concept suggests a system of specialization and mutual dependence. It encourages us to think of the global economy as one large production process divided up among nations, with each region or nation taking responsibility for one or more of the elements (goods and services) necessary to keep the whole in operation.

With this image in mind, economists since Ricardo have argued that the market organizes the division of tasks to take advantage of differences across regions in skills, endowments, and other capacities. Trade between regions and nations enhances overall efficiency.

This image might work well if specialization followed natural endowment. But, while consideration of natural capabilities is obviously relevant for some goods, the fundamental contours of international specialization and of global wealth and poverty are poorly explained by trying to apply this rule.

Much more important has been the rule of market size and market shares. Specialization follows competitive success. Regions specialize in manufactured goods, in high technology products, in financial services, not because of their endowments of resources but because of their historic success in competition over market shares in those industries. Their endowments result from past competitive success. Such success has much to do with institutional framework, past access to markets, and past accumulations of capital. What appears as a global division of labor is, on closer inspection, a global division of markets. The division of labor follows the division of markets rather than vice versa.

The idea of a global division of markets makes more sense the more the global economy consists of an integrated market system rather than a series of quasi-autonomous markets linked by a limited group of traded goods. The more we can speak of one global market, the more we must be concerned with the way shares of that market are divided among competing producers and among producers in different nations. The emergence of a more integrated market system goes hand in hand with a movement away from differentiation in economic structure across nations and regions and toward economic systems organized along similar lines and moving toward similar levels of development.

Labor costs and living standards

When we buy the produce of lower wage countries at a cost lower than we would pay if we produced the goods ourselves, we benefit from low wages paid in those countries.[12] If we can sell what we produce at a high price (i.e., under favorable terms of trade), we can benefit from our own high wages. When we buy goods under these conditions, in effect, we buy others' labor cheap and sell ours dear.

Eventually, however, the high price of our own labor becomes a competitive disadvantage for us. It does so when countries that pay lower wages develop the ability to produce some of the same goods that we produce at home at a higher cost. We can still buy the (produce of the) cheaper labor abroad, but when we do so, we forfeit the chance to sell our more expensive goods both home and abroad. As measured by standards of the world market, our labor is too expensive.

We can think of the cost of the cheapest labor available in the world market for producing a particular commodity as the *competitive price of labor.* If we pay our workers more than this without an offsetting advantage in productivity, our produce becomes expensive and eventually uncompetitive. When our goods become uncompetitive, the workers who were hired at the price that exceeded the competitive price of labor lose their jobs. This loss of jobs is the way the free market goes about adjusting wage costs to the competitive price of labor. The free market will do this automatically. In a world of free trade, we can continue to buy (the products of) cheap labor, but we cannot sustain the level of income associated with selling (the products of) our own expensive labor.

This creates a dilemma that a free market economy cannot resolve for us. We must choose between cheapening our own labor by adjusting its price toward the competitive world price and imposing limits on the way we participate in the world market. Because different nations are at different levels of economic development, and their peoples expect different living standards, the world market is always one in which products of labor bought at different prices confront one another. This confrontation does not always work to our advantage; we cannot always sell dear and buy cheap. When it works against us, the economic problem cannot help becoming a political one. In a real sense, the market fails to sustain our living standards. It threatens, instead, to adjust them to the competitive price of labor.

The problem is to bring our cost of labor into line with a cost determined

---

[12] This is a low cost in goods we produce and exchange for imports and thus depends on the terms of trade.

by a lower standard of living in another country. To do so, we can (1) import cheap laborers willing to work for a wage allowing a standard of living closer to that of our competitors, (2) drive down the living standards of our own workers, or (3) create a distinction between the wage we pay our workers, therefore their cost to producers, and their standard of living. The first two solutions pose significant social problems. Both challenge historically achieved levels of living that form a kind of subsistence as I define that above. This leaves the third alternative.

The third solution means socializing part of the costs of labor. When private industry must foot the bill for medical insurance for its employees, rising costs of medical care mean rising labor costs. If government subsidizes health care, the cost of labor to the firm diminishes (or rises less slowly). The principle, can, of course, be applied more broadly. Clearly, attempting to maintain living standards by socializing labor costs leads to a significant expansion of the government budget. Financing this solution to the problems of a maturing economy means a shift in the way we divide our incomes between the parts devoted to private and public ends (i.e., that part spent by the government rather than by the private citizen). This also shifts our standard of living by changing the mix of consumption in the direction of social expenditures.

Economic maturity raises an issue concerning the appropriate mix between private and public. Debate over this issue has been significantly hampered (especially in the United States) by the so-called tax revolt aimed at preventing exactly that shift demanded by a changing relation with the global political economy. In Part V I explore some of the underlying issues posed by our way of thinking about taxes. These issues are not simply about taxes and living standards but about the fabric of our lives together. They have to do with how we cope with the end of a long period of growth in productivity capable of sustaining rising living standards and how we distribute the income that we have in a period of economic maturity.

The prospect of socializing a set of expenses currently the responsibility of the individual (e.g., health care) challenges a basic premise of the private enterprise economy – that livelihood should depend on exchange. It does so by explicitly acknowledging that the wage serves two potentially conflicting functions: It is both a cost and an income. When conflict arises between these functions, we need to rethink the institutions of the wage system and consider possible modifications that redefine the link between the cost of labor and the standard of living of the laborer.

The government must, so far as possible, assure living standards where the market fails to do so. The global market does not know the appropriate standard of life for the citizen of a particular nation. The market can adjust cost and price so as to assure that full advantage accrues to the buyer from the lowest cost production available. But the buyer must also sell something. And circumstances arise, the world economy being one, in which the circle that connects buyer and seller favors the buyer at the expense of the seller when they are both in fact the same person.

12

International society

Obligations to others

When the global economy becomes the setting for pursuit of our private ends, the world of private affairs takes on boundaries different from those of public authority and responsibility. In the older language I allude to in the introduction to this book, the boundaries of civil society extend beyond those of the state. The modern world has moved rapidly in the direction of a global economy and global society. But the legal jurisdiction of the state remains geographically limited. This lack of concurrence between state and society poses an important problem (see Keohane and Nye 1977).

If there is no authority to regulate international conduct, does this make the world order a system of anarchy? Does the anarchic aspect of the global system discourage states and citizens from pursuing ends other than those rooted in their self-interest?

Those who study the political dimension of the international system emphasize dilemmas that arise due to its anarchic structure (Bull 1977). States exist and interact without any higher authority to enforce rules and patterns of conduct. Some argue that anarchy encourages each state to pursue its particular interests – in national wealth, power, and security (Waltz 1979). Whatever ties develop between states and between their citizens do so to serve self-regarding ends. Each state calculates its interest and takes those actions vis-à-vis other states most likely to achieve that interest.

Some authors explore the possibility that, underlying the anarchy implied in the absence of world government, there might exist an implicit order of mutual regard capable of supporting a kind of public, or common, purpose where no state or governmental authority exists (e.g., Kratochwil 1989; Nardin 1983). This might mean that we share links of right and duty even where we do not share citizenship. If so, our obligations to others do not end at our nation's borders. How obligations to others do or do not depend on shared citizenship becomes important.

In the global arena, the core issue of political economy – that of the relation between public authority and private interest – takes on significant new dimensions. International economic interdependence erodes the state's capacity to implement economic policy. Thus the global reach of private interest diminishes the capacity of the state with its more limited reach to accomplish public ends so far as those involve regulation of economic outcomes.

As I suggest in the previous chapter, the international economy can frustrate efforts of national governments to pursue economic policies aimed at improving domestic economic performance. If one government stimulates its economy while another engages in restrictive policies, the first will experience an increase in imports at the same time as the second reduces its demand for imports. The net result is a deterioration in the trade balance in the country attempting to stimulate economic activity.

If one country introduces measures aimed at protecting the environment while other countries adopt more relaxed policies, this can encourage producers to move their plants away from the ecologically minded nation. Income supports (unemployment insurance, welfare programs) set lower limits on wages and enhance workers' bargaining power. By so doing they can lead to higher wage scales that make domestic goods more expensive than those we might import from abroad. This can adversely affect our competitiveness and depress domestic demand and employment. The more dependent our economy on the global system, the less we can pursue economic policies on our own, and the more domestic policies of different countries must be coordinated to be effective.

But coordination often proves difficult. Policies can only be coordinated if mutually reinforcing policies exist that simultaneously serve the particular interests of each separate government. Underlying talk of policy coordination and international cooperation lies the vexing issue of the presence or absence of a convergence of interests. As we have seen, in a competitive economy, including a competitive international economy, some win and others lose. Often the winners and losers do not have the same interest.

Much depends on what we stand to win and lose. Perhaps the winners end up somewhat better off than the losers, while none ends up worse off than they would be under a policy of autarchy. Some who play professional sports win and make large incomes doing so. Others lose, and make less. But even the losers identify their interests with those of their sport. On a more basic level, all who play experience a commonality of ends.

But what if more is at stake? What if, in the case of professional sports, the losers are thrown out? They end up unemployed or poorly employed, possibly even condemned to a marginal existence in a dangerous and hopeless environment. If these are the stakes in the game we set up when we make livelihood depend on exchange, we should not assume that all those forced to play feel they have a common end.

Which sort of world is the global economy? Is it one in which, whether we win or lose, we gain something and, at least, keep alive our stake in the rules we play by? These rules organize international economic affairs into a world of competing particular interests. In the previous chapter I raise some questions about the likelihood that global free trade will serve the interests of all participants. I consider both the benefits and harms of trade and suggest some limitations on the validity of the currently fashionable celebration of its virtues. These limitations challenge the assumption of a common interest in global free trade.

During the 1970s many economists who doubted the mutuality of benefits in a system of free trade thought in terms of a New International Economic Order.[1] In this order, wealthier nations would agree to policies that encouraged the growth and development of poorer nations. Thinking along these lines followed a conviction that the wealthier nations bore some responsibility for the plight of the poor. Some argued that poor nations were that way due to exploitation by the wealthy.[2] But responsibility does not require such causation. We may accept responsibility because of a larger sense of common membership in a global human order where each naturally bears some responsibility for others.

As Arthur Lewis has pointed out, the part of the wealth of advanced economies attributable to a transfer of resources from poorer countries is not large. Accepting this conclusion does not deny a measure of exploitation. Transfer of wealth from poor to rich has occurred.[3] This transfer of wealth from poor to rich does not imply that the rich made the poor that way, or that the transfer of wealth is what keeps the poor poor. Clearly, it doesn't help. But it may not be the essential factor.

Even if wealthy nations did not make the poor nations poor, they may have a responsibility to address the problems of underdevelopment and global poverty. Beyond the argument that wealthy nations make their poor neighbors poor lies the claim of responsibility derived not from culpability but from obligation. Even if we did not make our neighbors poor, we may still have a responsibility to them. This raises a question about the ethical bonds of the global system. Do ethical ties connect us across state boundaries; and, if so, do they make doing something about global poverty our responsibility?

Economic analysis will not answer the ethical question. But it can help put that question into context by helping us judge what sorts of ethical obligations make sense given the way economic forces operate. Insisting on an obligation to eradicate poverty and suffering presumes the power to do so.

[1] For an evaluation, see Taylor (1982).
[2] For a survey of theories arguing along these lines, see Brewer (1992).
[3] An important recent example is the debt crisis (see Stewart 1985).

Economic arguments can help us judge the extent of our capacity to make a difference.

In thinking about this question, we need to be clear on our objective. We may be able to alleviate the suffering that results from famine in Africa but unable to alter the social and economic conditions that cause famine. There is a close analogy here with domestic antipoverty programs. What we do to lessen the suffering caused by poverty differs from what we do to remove the underlying causes of poverty. Providing those below the poverty line with additional income can move them above that line so that, in effect, they are no longer poor (see Smeedling 1992). But this will not alone enable the poor to alter the life circumstances that drove them into poverty in the first place.

Internationally, the scale of the problem defies even the effort to raise populations above the poverty line, which in any case varies in its meaning from one culture to another. But the more important issue has to do with the root causes and the role of wealthy countries in addressing them. What part can developed or wealthy countries play in the process that moves poorer countries from poverty to wealth? The responsibility of the wealthy depends on the nature of the problem and the source of the solution.

The problem alluded to in the last paragraph is the same one Adam Smith addressed in his work. What makes some nations rich, others poor? How can a country go about becoming wealthy or more wealthy?

In one sense, the answer to the question of what makes a nation wealthy is a simple one. Nations become wealthy by accumulating capital, encouraging the development of an infrastructure appropriate to profit making through investment in capital stock and assuring that incentives exist for innovation that might eventuate in the growth of labor productivity. These processes take place in the context of expanding markets. The size and growth of the market available govern the opportunities for accumulation and innovation, thus for growth in employment and incomes.

These processes are rooted in the freedom to pursue private gain through use of private property, especially in the means of production. In other words, the institutions we associate with capitalism or private enterprise have at least the potential to make the wealth of nations grow. This potential is most likely to be realized where incomes are growing and markets expanding.

I have tried to indicate that the process is not a simple one. It encounters difficulties along the way. It does not always work well in a context of minimum government and the broadest possible scope of private discretion. Capitalists and entrepreneurs are not always in a position to make the socially desirable decisions. Markets and market incentives often fail, or lead to unexpected and unwanted results. Funneling resources into what is, in the short run, the most profitable line does not necessarily enhance society's capital stock. Thus opening a poor country to an influx of credit from international financial markets might lead to investment in productive capital and thus to economic growth. But it could also lead to speculation in real estate in urban areas, driving up prices of existing assets rather than stimulating production of new ones. If the latter is the outcome, the influx of resources has perverse effects, so far as the process of economic development is concerned.

But the process is not a simple one in another sense. Though it may be true that the institutions of capitalism can bring about the development of wealthy society, it is less than obvious how we go about creating those institutions and assuring that they will channel resources in directions conducive to long run growth of productivity, incomes, and employment. Furthermore, it is not just a matter of appropriate institutions. It is also a matter of habits of thought and ways of life oriented around private property and the pursuit of private accumulations of wealth in the form of capital stock. And, finally, the process requires a framework sustained by a public commitment to support the market both as a legal system and as a functioning entity.

U.S. policy usually assumes that free trade is a necessary condition for economic development; and it often assumes that free trade is also a sufficient condition. Neither assumption is as strongly supported by evidence and analysis as our policy makers seem to believe. Eliminating barriers to free trade is rarely, if ever, enough. And, in many cases, it's the wrong thing altogether. The rhetoric of governments committed to free trade often ignores the complexities of the process. Nothing in our analysis of political economy suggests that minimal government involvement in the economy is the best, or even a very plausible, route to economic growth.

The U.S. government has been a strong advocate of policies that liberalize trade and minimize the role of government (Baldwin 1987). These policies normally involve reductions in the size of government, in its capacity to secure the welfare of citizens, and in the scope of public enterprise. Our insistence that developing countries reduce public expenditure or privatize public enterprises might satisfy our ideological needs, but past precedent and experience nowhere prove they will encourage rapid economic growth (see Griffith-Jones and Sunkel 1986).

The market does not spontaneously beget an appropriate institutional setting. Institutions appropriate to economic growth must develop; ways of life must change; markets must be encouraged, protected, and circumscribed. There is much for government to do if it takes its responsibility to secure the public good seriously.

Even when we know what sort of economic framework encourages the growth of wealth, this does not mean we know how to build such a framework where it does not yet fully exist, and in a national context very different from our own. The matter of national difference is important. It opposes our effort to remake other nations in our own image. It also stands in the way of our taking responsibility for underwriting the transition to wealthy society in countries other than our own. If this is the case, however, what can we say about our obligations to others?

To the extent that the transition to wealthy society is a matter of know-how and the financing of investment, the wealthier countries can provide meaningful aid for the poorer. But, to the extent that this transition is a matter of habits of mind, ways of life, and social institutions, the main dynamic for change must be internal rather than external. Adam Smith understood this when he insisted that what makes a wealthy society is not amassing wealth but gaining the knowledge of how wealth is made and building the institutions that embody that knowledge.

The matter is not so different when we consider problems of domestic poverty. Transfer of income will reduce poverty, and adequate transfers are a necessary part of a program to alleviate the suffering imposed by the state of being poor. But transfers will not alter the habits of mind or limitations of opportunity that encourage reproduction of poverty as a way of life.

At home, we debate what obligations we have collectively for the poor and disadvantaged. We consider programs to alleviate poverty, or to provide medical care, housing, and food, for those who cannot provide for themselves. We do so because of a sense that we are part of a larger community. To be sure, in the United States this is a minimalist sort of community. Still, the poverty of our fellow citizens is a problem for us. It is our problem, not just theirs.

Globally, we tend to see our obligations differently. That is, we perceive non-citizens differently than we see citizens because we have special obligations to the latter we do not have to the former. But why does citizenship define the end of obligation? Why have less regard for other nationals who are, after all, no less persons? Questions such as these take us some distance beyond the more limited concerns of political economy. This is not to say that they are irrelevant to political economy. But the study of political economy can only illuminate one corner of the problem. This is the corner in which we find a global civil society: the world of persons and their private ends that extends beyond the limits of state boundaries and thus state authority.

Global civil society

The emergence of a global civil society has two important implications. First, it erodes differences between persons tied to national identity. This can support movements toward convergence of rights and definitions of personhood across countries. It can make respect for personhood independent of national identity, calling into question the distinction between obligations to fellow citizens and obligations to others. Second, the development of a global civil society affects the capacity of government to achieve public ends and to satisfy obligations toward citizens. In exploring these matters, political economy has something to contribute to the discussion of obligation in a global arena.

The expanding boundaries of civil society challenge the scope and power of the state. The movement toward free trade zones alluded to earlier illustrates the difficulties we face in setting the balance between the two in a global context.

Within a free trade zone, each nation agrees to eliminate most restrictions on trade across borders it shares with other participants. This implies a reduction in the power of government. The more open the economy, the more limited the capacity of government to pursue domestic policy. Creation of free trade zones represents, then, an expansion of civil society at the expense of government and the pursuit of public concerns.

The promise held out by free trade zones poses a problem. By encouraging expansion of civil society beyond national borders, the free trade zone has two important implications. First, it intensifies the problem of lack of concurrence between the boundaries of government and economy. This can reduce the capacity of government to articulate and pursue a national agenda and national purpose so far as those involve economic goals. This also reduces the effective claims of citizenship because a weakened government can only respond effectively to a more limited set of obligations to its citizens. Eclipse of public power cannot but eclipse public obligations, as the latter cannot exist without the former. The less relevant state boundaries to economic affairs, the less relevant the state to economic affairs.

The second possible implication of free trade zones works in the opposite direction. Free trade zones bring an implicit expansion of the domain of citizenship. Economic intercourse that takes no account of the nationality of participants and treats all as equals implicitly extends certain claims of citizenship across national borders. These are the claims implied in respect for property rights and the kind of equality associated with exchange of property. Buying and selling in a world market assumes and helps to create elements of a common culture. To the extent that ways of life are lived through modes of consumption, when access to a world market means access to a universal mode of consumption, it means access to a common way of life. This commonality tends to work, however slowly, against parochial differences in culture and group identity. Erosion of such differences challenges the differential regard that accompanies the distinction between ourselves and others. Implicitly, then, both civil society and the claims of citizenship take on boundaries different from those of the state.

There may be virtues in this expansion of the domain of citizenship toward a kind of implicit global citizenry sharing duties and obligations. It overcomes the parochialism of national boundaries and the proclivity of nationals to deny respect to others. The expansion of civil society brings with it a potential erosion of the kinds of national differences that encourage denial of rights to outsiders and claims that fellow nationals are in some way special, thereby more deserving of our concern and respect.

But this implicit expansion of citizenship carries dangers. In particular, it sets up a conflict between what we have come to assume as duties and obligations of citizenship and the realistic capabilities of practical action (on the part of government). The duties and obligations toward others that come with shared citizenship do not mean much without the power to act according to those duties and expectations: to significantly reduce or eliminate poverty in other parts of the world, to provide universal benefits of wealthy society including education and health care, perhaps to redistribute income in the interests of global equity.

If we are powerless to provide the rights of citizenship to others, we cannot really consider them fellow citizens. And, yet, the expansion of civil society beyond the limits of the state reduces rather than increases the power of government to assure that the rights of citizens are respected, especially when those rights involve economic considerations. If we believe that public ends are important, and can only be pursued with public power adequate to direct economic affairs, free trade can pose a threat to welfare if it threatens the capacity of the public authority to define and pursue public ends.

The question of the regard we have for those beyond our borders is a timely one. It gains significance from the progressive weakening of the correspondence between the borders of economic and political affairs. In the end, the question of regard for citizens of other nations calls upon our understanding of the regard we have for our fellows. We might, then, reverse the question of why have less regard for those beyond our borders and ask: Why extend our obligation to all those we recognize as fellow citizens? Why not see the limits of our private worlds as the limits of our obligation? This is the question I begin to explore in Part V.

V

Individual and community

13

The limits of the market

Market failure

The market does not always succeed in accomplishing even those ends for which it is, so to speak, designed. It sometimes fails to utilize, or leaves underutilized, the human and nonhuman resources available. It does not always provide a livelihood for those capable of working and making a productive contribution. When the market fails, it leaves us less well off than we might be, although its purpose is to make us better off.

We cannot always count on the market to assure adequate levels of capital accumulation and economic growth. The market will stimulate economic progress, but it often does so unevenly. Some benefit, some do not. Some nations grow, others stagnate. Market successes often leave failures in their wake. Creation of the new can destroy the old. The human costs are often substantial.

When we live in a market economy, we depend on it for our livelihood. Some, however, lack the opportunity, education, character, intelligence, motivation, or skills needed to make their way in the market. For those lacking the qualities needed to participate fully, the market has nothing to offer but poverty and a sense of being left out. The market takes no responsibility for those left out; and in a sense it is not responsible. But even though the market may not be responsible, society is. Society decides collectively what use it will make of the market and how far it will go in making livelihood depend on exchange.

Even more than this, society, because it employs the market as the framework for want satisfaction, makes our well-being contingent on our success in the market. For many who fail, though the market is not responsible, our use of markets might be.

Decentralization of decisions decentralizes responsibility. Ideally, this leaves little responsibility in collective hands, most in private. The entrepreneur who purchases capital equipment to produce and sell a product is taking his or her chances. The consequences may be profit and riches, or they may be losses and poverty. The student who pursues a business degree rather than one in the liberal arts may gain a higher salary on graduation than his or her counterpart majoring in the humanities; but, again, he or she may not. In a market economy, you pay your money and you take your chances. By tying private decisions to private consequences, the market seeks to accomplish a striking social purpose. It makes us capable of responsibility for our actions and for the consequences those actions have for our lives: private lives, private responsibility.

This is a powerful idea that has liberated human potential, encouraged self-reliance, and enabled individuals to determine their life projects and act as centers of initiative in the world. But the consequences of private decisions taken in private interest are not always private. Contracts sometimes affect others not party to them. These others find their welfare affected by decisions they do not make. As I indicated, economists refer to these consequences for others as external effects, or externalities. They are the consequences of the interdependence we experience as a result of our lives together.

The market itself creates many of these effects. Specialization and division of labor make us dependent on a larger collective reality. Individual producers cannot sustain themselves alone. Each depends not only on those who buy from him or sell to him but also on the market system as a whole.

The market encourages interdependence, but it does not always deal with the consequences. When it fails to do so, as with air pollution or aggregate demand failure, government is often called on to look after the welfare of individuals and the integrity of the system of interdependence as a whole.

Market failures, of the various kinds briefly summarized here, help us define the role of government in relation to the economy. The kinds of failure touched on here fall into three interconnected but distinguishable classes:

1. *Problems of interdependence.* The market often fails to deal with the coordination of private decisions and with the external effects of private contracts. Coordination and externalities are the terms economists use to capture the implications of the fact that we live together. They are the economist's in some ways odd language for talking about the demands and implications of our collective lives, our being a part of a larger community.

2. *Problems of exclusion.* The market establishes conditions for participation that some in society cannot meet. These barriers to entry take on special significance when society uses markets as the prime institution for organizing the provision of needs. When livelihood depends on exchange,

those who do not meet the conditions for participation cannot acquire their livelihood.

3. *Problems of inequality.* Among those who participate, some fare better than others. Incomes vary according to criteria whose fairness and socially beneficial effects are debatable.

Economists sometimes speak of the limits of the market as "market failures." Markets sometimes fail to make us better off; they may even make us worse off than we might be without them. Knowing the limits of the market's competence helps us define the role of government, so far as government is capable of competent action where the market is not.

We might be tempted, in light of this conclusion, to make market failure the central concept for drawing the dividing line between government and economy, politics and economics. Drawing the line in this way will take us a significant distance toward resolving the problem of state intervention, determining where we stand on the great debate over the self-regulating market. The more the market is prone to failure, the greater the scope for government intervention. It is all a matter of frequency of failure.

The market failure approach takes us some distance, but also poses problems for us. These problems stem from the most general and powerful idea within the market failure portfolio, that of externalities. Externalities are the consequences of interdependence. If the kinds of interdependence that undermine the beneficial effects of markets exist only in relatively isolated cases, then externalities will also be limited, so that we will only find them in unusual, if not rare, circumstances.

The more limited the effects of our actions on those not party to them, the more the market retains a territory, somewhat diminished, but nonetheless substantial. But if interdependence is the rule rather than the exception, the externalities criterion for allocating territory between market and government may not leave much land for the market to cultivate.

I suspect that, without too great difficulty, externalities can be found in virtually all action undertaken by consumers and producers in a modern economy. If I purchase a yellow car, this can diminish the welfare of pedestrians who loathe the color yellow. Burning wood in my fireplace pollutes the air breathed by those who do not have fireplaces.

The Cincinnati Art Museum holds an exhibition of photographs by the noted artist Robert Mapplethorpe. Included in the exhibition are photographs deemed obscene by some members of the community. Given the ideals and values these members hold, the exhibition has an adverse effect, to their way of thinking, on the community itself. It harms the very fabric of collective life. Granted, no one need visit the exhibit who does not choose to do so. Does it follow that all consequences of the exhibition are purely private and are privately chosen? Clearly, this depends on how we introduce the fabric of the community into the calculation of individual well-being. Community well-being, somehow defined, is a part of the interdependence considered above.

When we live with others, the quality of our lives depends on the quality of our life together. If we treat our life together as a matter of choice, we can think of the community's effect on us as an effect we choose to experience or to avoid. We might choose on the basis of our expectations of a gain or loss in welfare when we inhabit or shun collective life and the interdependence it brings with it. But if living together is not a matter of choice, we cannot think about the community in this way.

If living with others is not a matter of choice, then our community's welfare is the framework of our own. How we lead our lives in private can have public consequences. Little, if anything, qualifies as really external. The fabric of interdependence is a part of our private lives. Because of this, in deciding what to treat as a part of public life and public responsibility, the externalities criterion will not serve us well.

How can we reconcile this fact of collective life with the aim of the market to enable us to define our own ways of life and take, individually and separately, responsibility for our actions, our accomplishments, and their effects on others? I have presented examples of interdependence to highlight a weakness in the market failure approach (centering on externalities) to assigning tasks respectively to government and to the private sector. This weakness has to do with the ubiquity of interdependence and thus external effects of private contracts. When all, or virtually all, private decision and action implicate others not party to the decision or action, appeal to externalities does not identify a subset of actions justifying government intervention.

How, then, are we to distinguish the private from the public? We make this distinction in order to protect the integrity of the individual by establishing a private space for him and in order to protect the collective. We cannot allow government to decide in all cases where private action has unintended and/ or uninvited consequences. Doing so would justify an intrusiveness of government beyond anything consistent with individual rights as we know them. Even armed with the notion of market failure, we must still decide when the consequences of our life together make leaving outcomes to private contract unacceptable.

Private and public

How can we decide which consequences of interdependence vitiate private solutions and which do not? What criteria can we use? In this section I briefly summarize three possible criteria. Each has something important to offer, though none alone will resolve the problem. The three are democratic process, equal opportunity, and equal regard.

Those who place their faith in collective decision making argue that we can resolve the matter of allocation of tasks between public and private by identifying a decision-making procedure. We can let the community decide how to draw the line between free market outcomes and government control. In a democratic community collective decisions replace market outcomes when the community so chooses. The community can choose to find Robert Mapplethorpe's photographs obscene and ban them, or it can choose not to.

But when we allow the community to choose as it will, how can we protect the integrity of the member? Does the member have only those rights the community chooses to bestow on him? Is interdependence sufficient justification to make private initiative subordinate to the will of the community?

We have good reason to protect members from the decisions of their community even if we believe the community is the framework of the life of the member. Popular referenda in the state of Colorado limit the rights of homosexuals and prevent the state from adequately funding public education. These are only two instances among many in which democratic processes endanger the integrity of the citizen.

Democratic procedure does not, in any case, answer the question of what criteria we use to decide which protections to afford the member. Even within the framework of collective decisions, we need criteria for deciding. In particular, we need criteria that instantiate the idea of respect for the integrity of the member and concern for the fabric of collective life. Identifying procedures does not solve the problem; it only provides an appropriate setting. The procedure cannot tell us if the collective has decided wisely. The collective no less than the individual observer must know how to decide. And if our collective decision-making process includes deliberation and the effort to reason together, it all the more demands criteria we can refer to in attempting to convince those with whom we disagree. Our problem remains.

The principle of equal opportunity provides guidance. To see how it might apply, let me reconsider for a moment one of the most fundamental ideas of modern day political economy. This is the idea that a relation exists between choice and welfare such that welfare improvement follows expansion of choices. Expansion of choices follows the use of markets and the increase in wealth.

Growth in the range of choice must, at least potentially, improve welfare. Should we decide to pass up a choice available to us, we are none the worse off; our welfare simply remains at the level it was in the absence of the new option. Should we opt to take up the new opportunity (voluntarily choosing it over others), this means that in our judgment we are better off exploiting that option than others available to us. Thus, in our own judgment, the availability of the option makes us better off.

I have no argument to make with this observation so long as it is not taken too far. By too far, I have in mind the kind of generalization of the principle that goes something like this: Increasing the choices available can make us no worse off but has the potential to make us better off; the opportunity to choose is an opportunity to increase our welfare, and whatever the government can do to increase choices must improve welfare. This generalization of the virtue of choice takes us into a troubling territory.

The troubling territory is one in which choice makes us worse off. It is the territory in which the end of government is to assure that we will not have to face certain kinds of choices. Indeed, unlike the market, one purpose of government is to protect us from choices that endanger our integrity.

The illiterate voter faces political choices and the right to make a political decision among alternatives he or she cannot judge. The unemployed worker without adequate job skills faces employment options none of which either offers adequate income or a meaningful job experience. The single mother of three young children who cannot afford day care faces the choice of leaving her children with inadequate care or not working. The long term unemployed may face the option of sleeping in a shelter or on the street.

Are we always better off if given additional choices? Enslavement is illegal in the United States even if you want to enslave yourself to another. If the law prohibiting slavery were repealed for cases of voluntary choice, the options available to us would expand. Does this make us better off? Does it improve the welfare of those who would voluntarily choose the option were it available? Polygamy is also illegal in the United States. Would those women, for example, who might choose to marry men already married be better off given the option of doing so? Do more choices mean greater freedom, improved welfare?

Clearly there are circumstances in which the economist's claims for choice are not compelling. This does not mean the economist is wrong in encouraging expansion of choice. But it does suggest that we can draw a dividing line between government and market if we can distinguish areas in which choice enhances freedom and welfare from those in which it harms both.

The areas of harm are all areas in which the choices, although voluntary in one sense, also express a failure of personal autonomy or integrity and thus, in another sense, are not voluntary. Such choices as those listed above are voluntary in that they imply no overt coercion by an individual or institution. The individual is, in Milton Friedman's phrase, "free to choose." Yet the person is not really free. And this fact suggests to us that we need to concern ourselves with the preconditions for free choice and self-determined action.

One way of interpreting equal opportunity centers on its importance in assuring that all members of society can acquire the prerequisites for self-determined action. These prerequisites include the education needed for participation both in economic and political life, the inner personal resources needed to value autonomous action and reject forms of personal enslavement (both implicit and explicit), the social resources needed to pursue employment and the framework of a welfare system required to assure that job choice does not involve the option of starvation or its near substitutes.

We can distinguish between government's responsibility and the responsibilities of the free market if we can define clearly enough the preconditions for autonomy and personal integrity. The responsibility of the government is to assure that those preconditions are met so far as possible for all members of society. We can resolve the problem of the dividing line between government and market if we understand that freedom to choose has three rather than two dimensions:

1. The right to choose that follows the right to own and dispose of private property and the right to pursue employment options.
2. The availability of options including those afforded in a wealthy society by markets and by the growth of wealth.
3. The capacity to choose that depends on development of personal resources of character and education and on the assurances that choice is not driven by desperation born of poverty and economic insecurity.

Economists too often lose sight of the third of these dimensions. The principle of equal opportunity speaks to this dimension of the problem of choice. It recognizes that choice has meaning only for those who have the capacity to choose (see Sen 1992, Chapter 2), and that government plays a role in assuring, so far as possible, that each citizen has that capacity. In doing so, government takes responsibility in certain areas (such as education and health care) away from the market.

An example may help to highlight the implications of the distinction between the capacity to choose and the right to do so. In recent years, conservative policy makers have taken up a policy orientation they call *empowerment*. The term empowerment, used in this context, refers to policies aimed at placing the fate of citizens (in this case those who have historically fared poorly) in their own hands. This is an appealing notion and one that carries forward the important idea that escape from poverty cannot be imposed from outside but must ultimately be accomplished by the poor themselves.

Yet the way the term empowerment has been used asks us to assume that placing the fate of the poor into their own hands is enough – that we do not need to concern ourselves with providing programs through which the poor can develop the capacities they need to take advantage of their "empowerment." That is, the policy equates power with provision of opportunities, not considering the other side of power, which is the capacity to take advantage of those opportunities.

Consider the application of this notion of empowerment to the problem of urban poverty. One of the most intractable problems facing policy makers in the United States has been that of poverty in the inner cities. Periodic episodes of civil unrest underscore the importance of the problem and the failure of policy (or the lack thereof) to change the life circumstances of many inner city residents.

During recent administrations, the idea of "enterprise zones" has gained popularity (Levitan and Miller 1992). The policy would provide tax breaks for industry willing to locate in core urban areas.[1] It assumes that tax incentives will stimulate investment, which will create jobs in blighted areas. This might make sense if workers in blighted areas have the skills demanded by the jobs investment in their neighborhoods might provide. But this assumption carries little weight. Clearly, if the unemployed lack job skills, tax breaks for industries in urban cores will do nothing to increase employment and incomes there and thus ameliorate the underlying problems. A policy aimed at free market solutions that empower private citizens to solve their own problems runs up against the limit of the capacities of those citizens to take advantage of those opportunities.

Equal opportunity speaks primarily to the matter of capacities. It says little about outcomes, outcomes having to do with the distribution of income and wealth. This silence on the matter of outcome can be both a strength and a weakness. It may be that we would consider inequalities of income and wealth justified so long as each of us had an equal opportunity to gain high income rather than low, and so long as the lowest income was not such as to threaten the basic integrity of the person. If we believe this principle, we might stop here in thinking about legitimate government intervention. Stopping here, however, leaves out an important consideration.

When inequalities of income and wealth progress beyond a certain point,

---

[1] Because of the politics involved, it does not work out in practice that the policy is nearly so well targeted at those areas where the need is greatest. Instead, each local constituency wants to benefit from designation as an enterprise zone because it can give that locality a competitive advantage in attracting business. The political momentum set up in this way tends to diffuse the policy's impact.

they may call into question the underlying equality of persons on which modern economic and political systems are founded. Those systems claim that all persons are created equal, and recognize a set of noneconomic rights that all possess equally. For example, although we may have different amounts of wealth, in principle we each have one vote; politically we are meant to be equal. Yet inequalities of wealth, once allowed to progress too far, can threaten this other dimension of equality and thus endanger the underlying equality of persons (see Lindblom 1977). We may each have one vote, but politically this has small significance next to the influence that wealth can bring to bear on political decisions. Here, economic inequality begins to threaten political equality.

The concept that speaks to this aspect of the problem is the concept of equal treatment. Regardless of our income and wealth, we expect to receive equal treatment in our lives together; we expect to be treated with the respect due us as citizens of a nation founded on the principle of equality.

We sometimes equate equal opportunity with equal treatment, but equal treatment also carries connotations that might take us further. It does so because it emphasizes how we act in relation to each other rather than simply eliminating inappropriate barriers to our action. I have elsewhere (Levine 1988) suggested some implications of a stronger version of the notion of equal treatment that I term equal regard. If we treat each other with equal regard, or attempt to do so, this has implications for how we draw a line between market and nonmarket solutions to problems of distribution.

By equal regard, I have in mind the idea that all citizens be considered equally persons and be treated equally as persons. Some of us are physically stronger than others, some have more talent for music or mathematics, some have more ambition. All of these differences are relevant to our life chances. For the government to attempt to override them flies in the face of any basic commitment to individual self-determination. Accepting these differences need not, however, imply accepting any given set of implications for income distribution those differences might have. The organization of the economy helps determine how differences such as these will affect our income and wealth. We can celebrate differences between persons in talents and accomplishments without creating a system of differential rewards.

When we allow the market to value differences of the kind indicated above, we wrap those differences into a scheme of differential income and wealth. In our society such differences carry implications for how we see ourselves in relation to others. To retrieve a theme introduced in Chapter 2, these differences become the basis for invidious distinctions between persons. These invidious distinctions rest on a connection between wealth and worth. We come to measure our worth as persons by our wealth. We celebrate differences in talents and accomplishments to the point of threatening our underlying commitment to the notion that we are all equally persons and to be treated equally as persons.

If we maintain a commitment to equal regard, and to equal treatment in order to maintain equal regard, then we can justify intervention to even out those differences in income and wealth that challenge our notion of equality. When differences in income and wealth reach the point where they mark different statuses, or even classes, of persons, they challenge the notion of equality. The notion of equal regard thus provides a criterion for limiting the market stronger than those provided by the notions of externalities or equal opportunity.

Integrity

The concepts of equal opportunity and equal regard place emphasis on individual integrity. They direct our attention toward the capacities individuals need to define, pursue, and achieve their ends. We can use these concepts to help us think about the limits of the property system and the obligations of government. The way we set the balance between public and private, allocating tasks to each arena, affects individual capacities and opportunities.

The externalities concept draws our attention away from the question of individual integrity and the conditions needed to enable individuals to define and achieve their goals. It does so by assuming that (1) individuals have the capacities needed to act effectively in a market-centered world, (2) attaining those capacities does not depend on public institutions, and (3) individual integrity is not at stake in the world of private affairs.

The externalities approach depends on the assumption that, while the private arrangements we enter into to achieve our private interests might affect our degree of satisfaction or happiness, they do not affect our ability to achieve satisfaction and happiness. The idea of integrity embedded in notions of opportunity and regard encourages us to wonder if the pursuit of private ends might sometimes endanger the individual's (and possibly the group's) integrity.

The idea of integrity can help us determine when externalities should become the concern of government and when they should not. When the external effects threaten the integrity of persons or groups not party to transactions, those persons and groups clearly have a significant stake.

Matters of private welfare become matters of public concern when private transactions either fail to secure welfare or possibly endanger it. This happens when those with a stake in outcomes can neither speak nor be heard. They cannot speak if they lack the capacity to do so: if they are illiterate, homeless, or lack hope for their futures. They will not be heard if their concerns have no forum. The market economy provides no forum for those who are affected by it but lack either the resources to participate or the opportunity to do so.

What can we conclude about the relation between private interest and public action? Put simply, the private world guards the integrity of citizens by assuring them the opportunity to use their property to pursue their own ends; the public authority guards the integrity of citizens by securing, so far as possible, their capacities for self-directed action, while protecting them from danger to their integrity resulting from the self-directed actions of others. Viewed in this way, public and private both center on individual freedom or self-determination. The balance of the two follows the distinction between securing capacities and exploiting opportunities given those capacities.

Political economy restricts its vision of public life to, at best, a vision of measures needed to secure capacities and opportunities. It does not extend the mandate of public affairs to include a public agenda aimed at goals rooted in the life people live together, collectively as a community. This need not mean that political economy must reject the possibility of public ends irreducible to protecting the individual's private welfare. It does mean that exploration of such ends takes us beyond the limits of political economy.

Political economy explores the balance of public and private within a framework defined by private welfare and the pursuit of private interest. In the last chapter of this book I consider some of the broader implications of the quest for private space that defines the basic concern of political economy.

14

Private ends, public good

Public ends

In a capitalist economy we each pursue our self-interest with little regard for the welfare of our fellows, who we assume are looking out after their own. The fact that we live together means, of course, that what we do affects others and that our success in achieving our ends depends on our fellows. This dependence can enhance our well-being, as when we can purchase from others the things we want but do not have. Dependence can also diminish our well-being when we are adversely affected by decisions and actions taken without our consent.

Political economy suggests that we think about our institutions as ways of minimizing harms and maximizing benefits of interdependence. The two most important sets of institutions are those associated with markets and with government. The market is meant to enable us to take advantage of each other's self-interest; government is meant to minimize the harms pursuit of self-interest poses for us and to deal with needs the market cannot satisfy or satisfy well.

In this view the aims of government do not differ in kind from those of the market: to enable us to enhance our private welfare, to achieve our private ends so far as possible, and to secure and safeguard our ability to define and pursue our interests. We conceive the ends of government and market in essentially the same way; they are to serve the private interests of individuals. Those interests are the benchmark of market success and failure and of desirable government intervention.

This interpretation of the ends of our institutions leaves little room for specifically group interests, that is, interests of the collective that are defined along dimensions other than that of private ends. The term traditionally used for such group interests is the public (or common) good. Political economy has tried to make us see the public good as the sum of the goods of

174

the private citizens. The better off we each are individually, the better off we are collectively.

The history of political economy is often interpreted along the lines suggested in the previous paragraphs. Beginning with Adam Smith, this is a history of theories aimed at educating us to see in the public good nothing more than the sum of individual welfares. And to a large extent political economy tries to teach us just this lesson. But when we view political economy this way we lose sight of a distinction between the classical economists and those who followed them. For the classical economists, there was a public good irreducible to the satisfaction of private ends. This was the public good of capital accumulation and economic growth.

Adam Smith thought that as a society we have a group interest in moving from the state of poverty to that of wealthy or civilized society. This was thought to be the appropriate goal of economic policy.

We might assume that, if economic development is a public good, it is also the responsibility of government. But, of course, it was the argument of the classical economists that economic development would best be served by allowing individuals to pursue their private interests with a minimum of government involvement. The classical economist considered civilized society the unintended consequence of self-seeking. This collective end was best accomplished without any explicit plan or intent. When the institutional framework allowed, the innate interest of each in his private well-being would lead to the accumulation of capital and the growth of social wealth.

This may not always be the case, and the free market might leave some nations stagnant and poor while making others dynamic and wealthy. Whether the free market works, or active government involvement is needed for economic development, development remains a public good in the sense suggested earlier. As such, we can debate whether it is the best and wisest end for our society to pursue. When we debate this we also debate the institutional arrangements we favor, because those that encourage development may not look so attractive on other grounds.

As we have seen, the institutions of private enterprise encourage individuals to pursue activities conducive to economic growth. An important part of the raison d'etre of capitalism is its inherent dynamism and orientation toward economic development. So long as we consider economic growth and development a paramount collective goal, the institutional arrangements of private enterprise make sense. The lower the priority we place on growth and development, however, the less compelling those institutions.

If we take economic development as a crucial example of the public good, it tells us something important about what that idea means to us. It refers to a direction we hope to move in as a society. If we have such a direction, we have a collective end whose achievement is the public good.

In our society collective ends or purposes tend to come in two forms. They either have to do with our shared ideal of the person and how we might assure that members live up to that ideal, or they have to do with the overall framework of our life together. That framework may involve a sense of membership in a larger whole or community, including a way of defining the larger social and natural environment we depend on in working to realize the ideals we value. Before returning to questions of the greater framework of our collective lives, let me explore the idea of public end that has motivated political economy over the past three hundred years. This is the ideal bound up with the process of economic development.

Ways of life

How can we best characterize economic development, and what makes it a public good? Clearly, a developed economy has the capacity to generate more income and wealth, both overall and per person. By so doing, a developed economy can provide a higher standard of living for most if not all of its citizens. In Part II of this book I explored some of the mechanisms by which the process of economic growth increases incomes and raises living standards.

Today, most of us take for granted the advantages of the higher standard of living our economies provide for us. Put another way, our standard of living defines our way of life; the things we want and normally have all play a part in how we lead our lives. To lose many of them would mean to change how we live. In this simple sense, to give up the fruits of economic development would mean a loss. But this is a loss of a way of life, and it is not inappropriate to ask: Do we value our way of life simply because it is ours or does it sustain fundamental human values important in themselves? Do automobiles, televisions, private homes, quality health care, and so on satisfy important human purposes, or are they simply the artifacts of a particular culture, meaningful to us because it is ours, but of no larger importance?

This question poses a challenge to the process of economic development whose virtue is that it has made possible the way of life we enjoy. As we have seen, development also has its costs. Thus, why we value our way of life bears on how we judge development as a public good.

I do not think it relevant here to make arguments about particular of our cultural artifacts and the form means of consumption take for us: the kinds of automobiles we drive or the virtues of private versus public transportation, detached houses versus apartments, how we prepare our food and the kinds of food we prefer. Nations and cultures tend toward intolerance on matters such as this, interpreting difference as inferiority. In the modern world cultural chauvinism seems inseparable from cultural difference. This raises important issues concerning the virtues of ways of life and the limits of difference. I will not address those issues here.

There is, however, an issue about ways of life I would like to address, that of the part played by wealth in supporting those ways of life consistent with individual freedom. Is there a connection between wealth and freedom such that we can take a measure of wealth as a prerequisite to freedom? If so, how do we determine that measure of wealth? Is there something about the way of life afforded by wealth that makes freedom possible and economic development a public good?

In order to answer these questions, it will be helpful to consider some of the vital dimensions of the way of life afforded by the wealth available in a developed society. Here I consider two broad dimensions: security of the person and choice and opportunity.

Wealth can be used to enhance individual security in a number of ways. The most obvious of these are nutrition and health care. It is costly to maintain our physical capacities at their highest levels, and more costly the older we become. The wealthier our society, the better we can afford these costs and thus the more secure we are in regard to our physical well-being.

A wealthy society also has a capacity to secure material well-being.[1] Its greater productive capacity and greater control over natural forces make it possible to overcome the vicissitudes of welfare that result from closer dependence on the natural cycle and the accidents of weather and fertility. It does not follow, as we have seen, that our livelihood is in fact more secure in wealthy society. When wealth is privately owned, and our access to it depends on the value of our capacities in the market, our material well-being is anything but secure. But it could be. Society certainly has the material means to secure well-being, and wealth has much to do with that fact. How we use wealth may or may not make us more secure than we would be without it.

Beyond security, wealth creates choice and opportunity. For many of us, wealth means liberation from monotonous, alienating, and spirit deadening labor. With increases in the productivity of labor, a smaller and smaller part of the population is relegated to the tedium of laboring in the older sense. A larger and larger part can find work that challenges the intellect, provides scope for creativity, and expresses the individual's talents and capacities. Clearly we have far to go in spreading this opportunity throughout the work force. But our wealth has much to do with the remarkable expansion of outlets for creative energy in work.

[1] David Ricardo noted this virtue of wealthy society in a somewhat different connection when he argued that living at the bare subsistence "the people are exposed to the greatest vicissitudes and miseries" because in the event of a deficiency "of the chief article of their subsistence, there are few substitutes of which they can avail themselves" (1951, pp. 100, 101).

To take advantage of these opportunities, a measure of education is needed; and this has a substantial cost. Expectations of citizens regarding the kind and amount of education that will be provided grow steadily with the process of economic development. The needs of the economy for more and more educated workers lead to changes in those expectations. The costs of education are more easily borne the greater the wealth available. Here, also, wealth expands opportunity. Again, as we have seen, many continue to be excluded (see Burtless 1990). The wealth of society may or may not benefit any individual citizen. The limits and scope of public responsibility for education are currently a subject of heated debate. Yet, again, with the growth of wealth comes the expansion of possibilities. How we take advantage of them is another matter.

In the chapter on poverty I related poverty to deprivation of opportunity. Wealth can create poverty when it is distributed in a sufficiently unequal manner. But the poverty that wealth creates is the deprivation of the opportunities that wealth creates.

These opportunities center on expression and development of individual potentials, capacities, and interests. They are bound up with the things we do to establish our personal identity, or sense of self. We need wealth to do this. The classical thinkers emphasized the multiplication of needs that comes with the growth of wealth. This multiplication of needs and of the things that might satisfy them connects to multiplication of ways of life. In wealthy society it is possible for each of us to design our own way of life made up of the things we use or consume, the kind of work we do, our preferred leisure activities, and so on. The diversity of wealth is vitally important if we value the diversity of persons. The diversity of wealth makes it possible for persons to express and live out their differences.

Wealth makes choice of way of life possible. And this may be its most significant achievement. The connection of wealth to diversity of ways of life connects it directly to the value we place on individuality. A measure of wealth is needed, then, in a society dedicated to valuing individuality, self-determination, and self-expression.

Is economic development, then, a public good? It is if two conditions are satisfied: (1) if the economy is not developed, or sufficiently developed, to provide the wealth we need for the purposes outlined above, and (2) if we value individuality. The second point is, of course, vital. Economic development, understood as an objective of social policy, contains an implicit judgment and shared ideal about the kind of people we want to be and the kind of people we want to live with.

The notion of the public good has two dimensions: a goal or end toward which society intends to move involving an ideal, and a process to reach that goal. The public good is both process (development) and end (ideal). This division of the notion of the public good into two aspects leads to an important question. Are the values that define the end or ideal also those embodied in the process? More concretely, does the process of capital accumulation and economic development encourage and require us to act in the ways we would like to have people act given our motivating ideal?

I can make this point clearer by referring to incentives. How well the process of economic development works depends in part on the kinds of incentives society creates to encourage members to participate in and contribute to the growth of capital, productivity, and wealth. Socially defined incentives encourage us to be certain kinds of people. In the eighteenth and nineteenth centuries, economists emphasized the virtues of hard work and frugality. Hard work and frugality defined the social ideal, and, it was thought, the better we lived up to this ideal, the more productive we would be individually and collectively.

Yet, by their nature, frugality and hard work are virtues of a development process. They are virtues because they make us each work for the greater good, as Adam Smith defined it, of an increasing national revenue. This view seems to invert the relationship suggested between process and end. After all, the ideal of how we lead our lives was meant to be the goal, development the process of getting there. Here, however, the ideal of frugality and hard work derives from the process of development. This leaves us without a goal, or with the growth process as an end in itself. Something is not quite right.

The process of economic development requires us to institute an incentive system that makes our private ends work for a larger good, in an older language to harness self-seeking to the public interest in a growing national revenue. The most important single element of this incentive system has been the labor market. Throughout the pages of this book I have emphasized the way capitalism makes livelihood depend on the sale of the individual's capacities in the market. This dependence is the greatest incentive of all. We must work to live, and the work we do must be valued by others (as expressed in demand for our labor) for it to provide us with our living. We must adapt our ends, then, to the needs of the market.

We do this when we choose a career or profession on the basis of likely employment opportunities or income rather than on the basis of our sense of what would be most meaningful to us. When this happens the pursuit of self-interest need not mean self-determination. The disparity arises because we must have an interest in income and financial security. To serve that interest we may have to sacrifice self-determination – the pursuit of a life fashioned to exercise our talents, express our values, do those things that have meaning for us. How many students major in business administration whose real vocation is in music, art, or anthropology? The economic process utilizes the neediness of the individual to make him or her work for society, to make self-determination a molding of our lives to the external forces of the market.

There are virtues in this; but there are also problems. The process of economic development does not exhibit the same comfortable relation between wealth and freedom we envision as the end of that process. The end emphasizes self-determination and self-expression in choice of work and choice of the way we live. The benchmark or guiding factor is internal to us; we are led by the needs and interests of ourselves. The process requires that we mold those needs and interests in service of a process aimed at moving society in a particular direction.

Another way of making this point draws attention to the role of private property. Private property can be understood as both means and end. As means, it is part of the incentive system. The system of incentives that makes us all work for the growth of productivity and wealth requires that our capacities be our own property and that what we can get by using them also be appropriable by us.

To make us work hard, the economy offers rewards. But these rewards are private, or at least, they can be appropriated. We can share them if we want, but we do not have to; it is up to us. This is part of what we mean by private property. The incentive system and the goal it embodies of economic development require us to respect private property and to make as much of our social wealth private as is feasible.

But private property is also an end in itself, valued not because without it we would work less hard (or not at all) but because private property is part of the ideal of a way of life we think wealth will secure for us. That ideal includes for each of us a world of our own: of our own making and to which others enter only by our invitation. The term private refers to this world (or place) and to the way society recognizes the limitations of access to it. Private property refers to the things we acquire or create that frame our world. Our property gives our private space a special kind of reality, the kind we associate with objects. These objects are things outside of us that frame the space we live in. They are our private property.

We value private property, then, not only for the incentives it supports but also in itself. Without private property, we would have no place for ourselves. At various points I have referred to the measure of wealth we need to sustain our autonomy. This connection between wealth and freedom stems from the role private property plays as a support for freedom. We need a measure of wealth to secure a space for ourselves.

Valuing private property for this reason takes us in a direction different from that suggested by the link between property and incentives. One important difference has to do with the kind of property that takes center stage. When we focus attention on the implications of property for incentives, property in labor and capital have special significance. Private property in labor is an institutional necessity for distributing income and wealth through the labor market and thus in accord with the value of the individual's capacities in that market. The labor market creates significant incentives for each of us to mold our competencies to the needs of society as expressed in the market for labor.

Arguments for private ownership of capital also rest on its part in creating incentives. We judge private enterprise in large measure by its ability to assure a process of the growth of social wealth and of economic development, not because it is a part of the space we create for ourselves. Our capital stock might make us rich, but it is not the sort of thing that makes a private world for us.

Capital and labor are less significant as private property when the role of property is to create private space rather than private incentives. This is not to say that we can be more free if our labor belongs to someone else. But treating our labor as a commodity only enhances our ability to establish a place of our own when we must sell it to acquire the means to buy the things that establish such a place.

Private property in means of production plays an important part in shaping an incentive system centering on the accumulation of private wealth, both as an end in itself and as a means to economic development. This incentive system, because it is tied to economic development, is also bounded by the limits of economic development and the growth of wealth. As we approach those limits, it is natural that the argument for private property centering on incentives will seem less compelling, and that the argument centering on the space we construct for ourselves will take on greater importance. One of the great challenges we face as a society is knowing when we are, indeed, approaching those limits and how we should modify our social and economic institutions to take into account the shifting balance between the importance of incentives and the importance of assuring that each of us will have wealth enough to secure a place in the world for ourselves.

Community

Does the integrity of the community take precedence over individuals' wants? Or do the desires of individuals set the agenda for community? Since the end of the last century, economists have taken the lead in arguing that the purpose of community is to serve its members' wants. Some economists argue that the form and ends of government ought to be determined by the self-interest of the governed (Buchanan and Tullock 1962). This would mean that the group has no ends of its own and that members do not pursue interests derived from the community rather than from themselves. This modern-day liberalism denies any precedence the ends of community might have in shaping individual action.[2]

It is never difficult to discover self-interest in the political agendas of citizens. When the state of Colorado considered changing a law preventing grocery stores from selling liquor, it was not difficult to predict who would favor the change and who oppose it. Liquor stores distributed leaflets showing the danger to the public interest in allowing supermarkets to sell beer and wine. They argued that doing so would increase teenage drinking and traffic fatalities due to drunk driving. Whether valid or not, it is difficult to see the debate in terms other than the clash of private interests. Supermarkets saw no danger to the public good and much benefit from repeal of the law preventing them from selling alcoholic beverages.

Does this mean that the economists are right and that the most sensible way to understand the relation of individual to community is to treat the community as one means by which individuals achieve their private ends? Doing so requires us to assume that individual ends exist outside the group, that the group is not a necessary reference point for the individual and his or her interests.[3] This becomes a problem insofar as wants have a meaning that involves the connection of the individual to others. In Chapter 2 I emphasize what I term the relational element in wanting. There I suggest that what we want is a connection with others. When we want particular things, we really want the place in the world those things signify. We want to connect ourselves to the meanings things embody.

Defining the meaning of things is the work of society and culture (see Douglas and Isherwood 1979). The meaning we take on in using things originates in the group, not in ourselves. We want what we want in order to establish our place in the group and provoke a group sense of who we are.

This relational element in wanting makes it more reasonable to think that the group might have some precedence over the member and that the member might have an interest in the group as something more than a means to his or her private ends. It also implies that our private ends compel us to reach out to others and to the community as a whole. Our self-interest is an interest in connection with others.

We may, of course, be more or less aware of this quality of wanting and interest. The less aware we are of the way our wants lead us to others, the less we value the community as a whole and the less well we incorporate its ends in our own.

Public radio and television are good examples of the complex relation

---

[2] For a discussion of liberalism, see Dworkin (1978) and Unger (1987).
[3] Hegel (1951, pp. 156–57) makes this point in a critical comment on Rousseau.

between public and private ends. Private communications networks respond to viewers' preferences as expressed in ratings and the amounts advertisers will pay for commercial time. If we had only private networks then all communication over television and radio would be determined by an economic calculation. Private interests would dominate.

Public television and radio exist, in part, because we believe that other ends are important in the way we communicate as a society. This communication can help sustain dimensions of our culture that might otherwise wither: serious, in depth news coverage, educational programming, minority cultural expressions, "high" culture that we value not because citizens have an interest but perhaps because we think they ought to. Public television and radio can express aspirations we have as a group that individually we might not see clearly or pursue actively.

When what we aspire to rather than what we are is at stake, economic calculations based on private interest come out wrong. If, indeed, the group is the framework and reference point for private ends, then we need a way of engaging as a group and thinking through the direction in which we will go as a community (see Durkheim 1958).

In Chapter 2 I discuss some of the ways in which what we think we want might differ from what will bring us satisfaction. Not only, however, can what we want differ from what we think we want, it can also differ from what we think we ought to want. Our interest in collective ends makes the ethical element in want explicit. This element disappears when we assume that we want what we want or that wanting is simply our visceral attraction toward things in the world.

The integrity of the group is the integrity of the environment that sustains the member. The ethical element in wanting clearly orients us toward the larger social and natural environment. It requires us to think about what we want and makes our ideas about ourselves and our world determinants of what we want.

In an interesting exploration of the health hazards of consumption, Ross Zucker (1993a) argues that we think differently when we place ourselves explicitly in a group context, thinking about what is good or right rather than simply seeking what we want. Zucker notes that decisions made for the collective tend to exhibit greater deliberation, a higher level of abstraction, to be more other-regarding, and to be more rational in the sense of taking more into consideration than matters of taste.

Zucker found that people will buy goods they consider harmful and believe they ought not to buy. Citizens often favor government regulation that imposes their own better judgment on themselves. Examples include individuals who knowingly purchase goods whose consumption or production endangers the environment (such as wood burning stoves), and others who buy canned tuna while supporting government restrictions on tuna fishing to protect dolphins.

Economists have interpreted the disparity between what individuals deem the public good and what they do individually in a different direction than that outlined here. They argue that the difference arises because individuals understand that their action will not affect collective outcomes (see Caporaso and Levine 1992, Chapters 4 and 6; Olson 1965). This means that what is rational for individuals when acting collectively (refraining from eating canned tuna) may not be rational when they act individually. Those who refrain from consuming canned tuna will not save the dolphins. They only deprive themselves of the satisfaction (such as it is) from eating canned tuna.

For the economist, the problem, then, is not that individual and collective ends differ; it is not that greater deliberation or regard for others might help determine what citizens want or value. It is that difficulties arise in pursuing private ends when those ends can only be achieved if pursued simultaneously by many persons. For those influenced by the economist's way of thinking, the community always and only serves private ends.

It matters whether we think that the community affects what and how we want, or simply the calculation we make in the effort to satisfy our wants. It matters whether we consider the social and natural environment that sustains us a part of ourselves and therefore a vital dimension of what we want, or a mere means to our ends. It matters whether our interest in ourselves is inherently, if often implicitly, an interest in our relations with others, or an interest without regard to others. If we lose the relational element in wanting, we also lose the idea that what we want for ourselves may be to live in a world of mutual regard, to pursue life projects that express our sense of self and mark a difference from others that has cultural significance and respects the reality of our life together.

References

Adams, John W. 1973. *The Gitskan Potlatch: Population, Flux, Resource Ownership, and Reciprocity.* Toronto: Holt, Rinehart, and Winston.

Appleby, Joyce. 1984. *Capitalism and a New Social Order.* New York: New York University Press.

Baldwin, Robert. 1987. "The New Protectionism: A Response to Shifts in National Economic Power." In Dominick Salvatore, ed., *The New Protectionist Threat to World Welfare.* New York: North Holland.

Baran, Paul. 1957. *The Political Economy of Growth.* New York: Monthly Review Press.

Bernstein, Michael A. 1987. *The Great Depression: Delayed Recovery and Economic Change in America, 1929–1939.* New York: Cambridge University Press.

Bhaduri, Amit. 1986. "Forced Commerce and Agrarian Growth." *World Development* 14:2 (February), 267–72.

Blecker, Robert. 1992a. "The Great Mercantile Republic: Adam Smith's Theory of Absolute Advantages and the International Division of Labor." Unpublished manuscript.

———. 1992b. *Beyond the Twin Deficits.* Armonk, N.Y.: M. E. Sharpe.

Bollas, Christopher. 1989. *The Forces of Destiny.* London: Free Association Books.

Brewer, Anthony. 1992. *Marxist Theories of Imperialism,* 2nd ed. London: Routledge.

Buchanan, James M., and Gordon Tullock. 1962. *The Calculus of Consent.* Ann Arbor: University of Michigan Press.

Bull, Hedley. 1977. *The Anarchical Society: A Study of Order in World Politics.* New York: Columbia University Press.

Burtless, Gary, ed. 1990. *A Future of Lousy Jobs?* Washington, D.C.: Brookings Institution.

Capdevielle, Patricia. 1991. "Foreign Labor Developments." *Monthly Labor Review,* August.

Caporaso, James, and David Levine. 1992. *Theories of Political Economy.* Cambridge: Cambridge University Press.

Chamberlin, Edward H. 1933. *The Theory of Monopolistic Competition.* Cambridge, Mass.: Harvard University Press.

Chasseguet-Smirgel, Janine. 1985. *The Ego Ideal.* New York: Norton.

Clark, John B. 1965. *The Distribution of Wealth.* New York: A. M. Kelley.

Clinton, William, and Al Gore. 1992. *Putting People First.* New York: New York Times Books.

Cooper, Richard N. 1972. "Economic Interdependence and Foreign Policy in the Seventies." *World Politics* 24:2 (January), 159–81.

De Marly, Diana. 1990. *Dress in North America.* New York: Holmes and Meier.

Dobb, Maurice. 1973. *Theories of Value and Distribution Since Adam Smith.* Cambridge: Cambridge University Press.

Douglas, Mary, and Baron Isherwood. 1979. *The World of Goods.* New York: Norton.

186   *References*

Dreze, Jean, and Amartya Sen. 1989. *Hunger and Public Action.* Oxford: Oxford University Press.

Durkheim, Emile. 1958. *Professional Ethics and Civic Morals.* Trans. Cornelia Brookfield. Glencoe, Ill.: Free Press.

Dworkin, Ronald. 1977. *Taking Rights Seriously.* Cambridge, Mass.: Harvard University Press.

1978. "Liberalism." In Stuart Hampshire, ed., *Public and Private Morality.* Cambridge: Cambridge University Press.

Ellwood, David. 1988. *Poor Support.* New York: Basic Books.

Finley, M. I. 1973. *The Ancient Economy.* Berkeley: University of California Press.

Friedman, Milton. 1962. *Capitalism and Freedom.* Chicago: University of Chicago Press.

Friedman, Sheldon. 1992. "NAFTA as Social Dumping." *Challenge,* 35:5 (September–October), 27–32.

Gordon, David. 1986. "Do We Need to Be No. 1?" *Atlantic Monthly,* April, pp. 100–108.

Griffith-Jones, Stephany, and Osvaldo Sunkel. 1986. *Debt and Development Crises in Latin America: The End of an Illusion.* New York: Oxford Unviersity Press.

Harcourt, G. C. 1972. *Some Cambridge Controversies in the Theory of Capital.* Cambridge: Cambridge University Press.

Hayek, Friedrich H. 1945. "The Use of Knowledge in Society." *American Economic Review,* September, pp. 519–30.

Hegel, G.W.F. 1951. *Hegel's Philosophy of Right.* Tr. T. M. Knox. Oxford: Oxford University Press (1821).

Heilbroner, Robert. 1985. *The Nature and Logic of Capitalism.* New York: Norton.

Hooker, Richard J. 1981. *Food and Drink in America: A History.* New York: Bobbs-Merrill.

Joffe, Walter G., and Joseph Sandler. 1987. "Adaptation, Affects, and the Representational World." In Joseph Sandler, *From Safety to Superego.* New York: Guilford (1968).

Jonaitis, Aldona. 1991. "Chiefly Feasts: The Creation of an Exhibition." In Aldona Jonaitis, ed., *Chiefly Feasts: The Enduring Kwakiutl Potlatch.* New York: University of Washington Press.

Journal of Income Distribution. 1992. *Special Issue on Subsistence.* David Levine, ed., Summer.

Kaldor, Nicholas. 1985. *Economics Without Equilibrium.* Armonk, N.Y.: M. E. Sharpe.

Kalecki, Michal. 1965. *Theory of Economic Dynamics.* New York: Monthly Review Press.

1969. "Money and Real Wages." In Michal Kalecki, *Studies in the Theory of Business Cycles.* New York: Augustus Kelley (1939).

Keohane, Robert, and Joseph Nye Jr. 1977. *Power and Interdependence: World Politics in Transition.* Boston: Little, Brown.

Keynes, John Maynard. 1936. *The General Theory of Employment, Interest, and Money.* New York: Harcourt, Brace, and World.

Koechlin, Timothy, and Mehrene Larudee. 1992. "The High Cost of NAFTA." *Challenge* 35:5 (September–October), 19–26.

Kohut, Heinz. 1977. *The Restoration of the Self.* New York: International Universities Press.

Krasner, Stephen. 1978. *Defending the National Interest.* Princeton, N.J.: Princeton University Press.

Kratochwil, Friedrich. 1989. *Rules, Norms, and Decisions.* Cambridge: Cambridge University Press.

Krugman, Paul. 1991. *Geography and Trade.* Cambridge, Mass.: MIT Press.

and Maurice Obsfeld. 1992. *International Economics,* 2nd ed. New York: HarperCollins.

Levine, David P. 1977. *Economic Studies.* London: Routledge.

1981. *Economic Theory,* Vol. II. London: Routledge.

1983a. "Two Options for the Theory of Money." *Social Concept* 1:1 (May), 20–9.

1983b. "How Economists View Policy." *Democracy* 3:3, 83–93.

1988. *Needs, Rights, and the Market.* Boulder, Colo.: Lynne Rienner Publishers.

Levitan, Sar, and Elizabeth Miller. 1992. "Enterprise Zones Are No Solution for Blighted Areas." *Challenge* 35:5 (May–June), 4–8.

Lewis, W. Arthur. 1978. *The Evolution of International Economic Order.* Princeton, N.J.: Princeton University Press.

Lindblom, C. E. 1977. *Politics and Markets: The World's Political-Economic Systems.* New York: Basic Books.

Lurie, Alison. 1981. *The Language of Clothes.* New York: Vintage Books.

Marx, Karl. 1848. *The Manifesto of the Communist Party.* In Robert Tucker, ed., *The Marx-Engels Reader.* New York: Norton, 1972.

——— 1967. *Capital,* Vol. I. New York: International Publishers (1867).

McNulty, Paul J. 1968. "Economic Theory and the Meaning of Competition." *Quarterly Journal of Economics* 82:4, 639–56.

Minsky, Hyman. 1975. *John Maynard Keynes.* New York: Columbia University Press.

Nardin, Terry. 1983. *Law, Morality, and the Relations of States.* Princeton, N.J.: Princeton University Press.

Nell, Edward. 1988. *Prosperity and Public Spending.* Boston: Unwin Hyman.

Nordhaus, William D. 1991. "The Cost of Slowing Climate Change." *Energy Journal* 12:1, 37–65.

Nozick, Robert. 1974. *Anarchy, State, and Utopia.* New York: Basic Books.

Offe, Claus. 1984. *Contradictions of the Welfare State.* Cambridge, Mass.: MIT Press.

Okun, Arthur. 1975. *Equality and Efficiency: The Great Trade-Off.* Washington, D.C.: Brookings Institution.

——— 1981. *Prices and Quantities.* Washington, D.C.: Brookings Institution.

Olson, Mancur, Jr. 1965. *The Logic of Collective Action.* Cambridge, Mass.: Harvard University Press.

Phillips, Kevin. 1990. *The Politics of Rich and Poor.* New York: Harper Perennial.

Polanyi, Karl. 1944. *The Great Transformation.* Boston: Beacon Press.

——— 1957. *Trade and Market in the Early Empires.* Chicago: Henry Regnery.

Rawls, John. 1971. *A Theory of Justice.* Cambridge, Mass.: Harvard University Press.

Ricardo, David. 1951. *The Principles of Political Economy and Taxation.* In *The Works and Correspondence of David Ricardo,* Vol. I, ed. Piero Sraffa. Cambridge: Cambridge University Press (1817).

Robinson, Joan. 1966. *The New Mercantilism.* Cambridge: Cambridge University Press.

Rosenberg, Nathan, ed. 1971. *Perspectives on Technology.* Cambridge: Cambridge University Press.

——— 1976. *The Economics of Technological Change.* Harmondsworth: Penguin.

Rowthorne, Robert. 1980. "Conflict, Inflation, and Money." In Robert Rowthorn, *Capitalism, Conflict, and Inflation.* London: Lawrence and Wishart.

Sahlins, Marshall. 1972. *Stoneage Economics.* Chicago: Aldine.

Sawhill, Isabel V. 1988. "Poverty in the U.S.: Why Is It So Persistent?" *Journal of Economic Literature* 26 (September), 1073–119.

Schelling, Thomas C. 1984. "Economic Reasoning and the Ethics of Policy." In Thomas Schelling, *Choice and Consequence.* Cambridge, Mass.: Harvard University Press.

Schumpeter, Joseph. 1934. *The Theory of Economic Development.* Cambridge, Mass.: Harvard University Press.

——— 1950. *Capitalism, Socialism, and Democracy,* 3rd ed. New York: Harper & Row.

Sen, Amartya. 1987. *The Standard of Living.* Cambridge: Cambridge University Press.

——— 1992. *Inequality Reexamined.* Cambridge, Mass.: Harvard University Press.

Shafer, Roy. 1983. *The Analytic Attitude.* New York: Basic Books.

Shapiro, David. 1981. *Autonomy and Rigid Character.* New York: Basic Books.

Smeedling, Timothy M. 1992. "Why the U.S. Antipoverty System Doesn't Work." *Challenge* 35:1 (January–February), 30–5.

Smith, Adam. 1937. *The Wealth of Nations.* New York: Modern Library (1776).

Steindl, Josef. 1952. *Maturity and Stagnation in American Capitalism.* Oxford: Blackwell.

Steuart, Sir James. 1966. *An Inquiry Into the Principles of Political Economy.* Edinburgh: Oliver and Boyd (1767).

Stewart, Frances. 1985. "The International Debt Situation and North-South Relations." *World Development* 13:2 (February), 191–204.

Sweezy, Paul. 1942. *The Theory of Capitalist Development.* New York: Monthly Review Press.

Taylor, Lance. 1982. "Back to Basics: Theory for the Rhetoric in North-South Round." *World Politics* 10:4 (April), 327–35.

Thayer, Warren. 1990. "The Time Bomb in Your Store." *The Progressive Grocer,* December, pp. 73–80.

Unger, Roberto M. 1987. *Social Theory: Its Situation and Its Task.* Cambridge: Cambridge University Press.

U.S. Bureau of the Census. 1992. *Statistical Abstract of the United States: 1992,* 112th ed. Washington, D.C.

U.S. Department of Commerce, International Trade Admininstration. 1992. *U.S. Foreign Trade Highlights 1991.* Washington, D.C.

   Bureau of the Census. 1975. *Historical Statistics of the United States: Colonial Times to 1970.* Bicentennial Edition, Part 2. Washington, D.C.

Veblen, Thorstein. 1899. *The Theory of the Leisure Class.* London: Macmillan.

Vernon, Raymond. 1966. "International Investment and International Trade in the Product Cycle." *Quarterly Journal of Economics* 80:2 (May), 190–207.

Walsh, Vivian, and Harvey Gram. 1980. *Classical and Neoclassical Theories of General Equilibrium.* New York: Oxford University Press.

Waltz, Kenneth. 1979. *Theory of International Politics.* Reading, Mass.: Addison-Wesley.

Winfield, Richard D. 1988. *The Just Economy.* London: Routledge.

Winnicott, D. W. 1965. "Ego Distortions in Terms of True and False Self." In D. W. Winnicott, *The Maturational Process and the Facilitating Environment.* New York: International Universities Press.

Zucker, Ross. 1993a. "Unequal Property Right and Subjective Personality in Liberal Theories." *Ratio Juris* 6:1 (March), 86–11.

   1993b. "Social Decision: Answer to Market-Made Health Crisis." Unpublished manuscript.

Index